THE BACKWARD-FLOWING METHOD

THE SECRET OF LIFE AND DEATH

JJ SEMPLE

A Life Force Books Publication

Disclaimer: The information in this book is for educational purposes only and is not intended as medical advice. Neither the author nor the publisher of this work will be held accountable for any use or misuse of the information contained in this book. The author, the publisher, and/or the distributors of this book are not responsible for any effects or consequences from the use of any suggestions, recommendations, or procedures described hereafter.

The author made all reasonable efforts to contact all literature sources quoted in the text.

Life Force Books
PO Box 302
Bayside, CA 95524
www.lifeforcebooks.com

ISBN: 978-0-9795331-2-9

Printed in the United States of America

THE BACKWARD-FLOWING METHOD

THE SECRET OF LIFE AND DEATH

The opinion of 10,000 men is of no value if none of them know anything about the subject.

~ Marcus Aurelius

TO GOPI KRISHNA

The experiments, besides providing indisputable evidence for the existence of design in creation, would at the same time open to view a new and healthy direction designed by nature for the sublimation of human energy and the use of human resources, frittered away at present in frivolous pursuits, debasing amusements, and ignoble enterprises unsuited to the dignity of man. The knowledge of the safest methods for awakening Kundalini and their empirical application on themselves by the noblest men physically and mentally equipped for it, will yield for humanity a periodic golden crop of towering spiritual and mental prodigies who, and who alone, in the atomic age will be able to discharge in a proper manner, consistent with the safety and security of the race, the supreme offices of the ministers of God and the rulers of men.

-Kundalini: The Evolutionary Energy in Man – Gopi Krishna

CONTENTS

HIDDEN IN PLAIN SIGHT

An ancient adept said: 'Formerly, every school knew this jewel, only fools did not know it wholly.' If we reflect on this we see that the ancients attained long life by the help of the seed energy present in their own bodies, and did not lengthen their years by swallowing this or that type of elixir. But the worldly people lost the roots and clung to the treetops.[1]

~ *The Secret of the Golden Flower* – Lu Yen - Richard Wilhelm, Translator

The backward-flowing method refers to a meditation technique mentioned throughout *The Secret of the Golden Flower*, a compilation of 8th Century meditation practices. First translated from the original Chinese and published in England in 1931, the book has been an off-and-on best seller, a fact that, in and of itself, is largely puzzling.

True, the book is important to the meditation tradition. But why it's remained so popular is curious, especially since its vaunted Secret Teachings, though implicitly advertised in the title, have never been adequately explained. Why do I say that the Secret Teachings have never been explained? I say this because the Secret Teachings in the *Golden Flower*—and there are many—are the actual Secrets of Life. That's right—as in Ponce de Leon's Fountain of Youth type of secrets. Secrets of monumental consequence. I believe these Secret Teachings, like the clues in some tangled mystery, may have escaped the discerning eye by the very fact that they are hidden in plain sight. If they had been adequately explained, these secrets would be common knowledge, their techniques applied in every strip mall Yoga class across the country. But they're not.

Perhaps part of the answer lies in the *cold case* aspect: the fact that after 1,200 years, tastes change. Nowadays, meditation partakes of the *Spirituality Made Easy* attitude, so prevalent in today's New Age culture. Twelve hundred years ago, a novice had to trek off in search of a Master. He had to be accepted, frequently only after undergoing a series of harsh trials. Finally, he was put through a spiritual boot camp. Today, one has only to drive into a strip mall to be propositioned by an assortment of New Age dojos, ateliers, and Yoga studios. It's a situation of supply and demand. Twelve hundred years ago, conditions were harsh; today, there's an oversupply of shortcuts to *Nirvana*.

Nevertheless, despite the changing times, *The Secret of the Golden Flower* has become part of the spiritual canon. Having it on the bookshelf is like having a copy of the *I Ching*—an item to be appreciated for its reputation rather than its true worth.

One would hope the real reason the book has remained popular is because any book purporting to hold the Secret of Life is bound to generate interest. However, most readers hear about the book, take a crack at it, then give up. Consider the following discussion from an online chat room:

23rd October 2007, 12:52 PM #1

SGW: Regular

The Secret of the Golden Flower

Anyone read this?

_____

25th October 2007, 07:42 AM #2

TK: Super Moderator

Re: The Secret of the Golden Flower

Portions of it—it's on my "to purchase/read" list, once I get a chance.

_____

29th October 2007, 10:28 AM #3

SGW: Regular

Re: The Secret of the Golden Flower

It is difficult to penetrate; I started back at the commentaries which was a lot of reading before you even get to the material.

For a small book, it's a tough read.

_____

7th November 2007, 07:54 AM #4

TR: Junior Member

Re: The Secret of the Golden Flower

So, what is the SECRET?

_____

7th November 2007, 10:49 AM #5

TK: Super Moderator

Re: The Secret of the Golden Flower

Quote: It is difficult to penetrate; I started back at the commentaries which was a lot of reading before you even get to the material.

For a small book, it's a tough read.

Yes, like many *neidan* or "Inner Alchemy" texts it uses a complex system of poetic imagery sometimes called "correlative cosmology"; much of the language and concepts are also used in TCM (Traditional Chinese Medicine). Very difficult stuff for the uninitiated; personally, I have only a very rudimentary understanding of it, and I've never attempted to read the whole of the *Flower*.

TR, it's an ancient Chinese manual on meditation, philosophy and self-cultivation, but it's couched in highly metaphorical/allegorical language. To give you an example, here's an online translation: *T'ai I Chin Hua Tsung Chih*.

16th November 2007, 11:11 AM #6
TR: Junior Member
Re: The Secret of the Golden Flower
Quote: Yes, like many *neidan* or "Inner Alchemy" texts it uses a complex system of poetic imagery sometimes called "correlative cosmology"; much of the language and concepts are also used in TCM (Traditional Chinese Medicine). Very difficult stuff for the uninitiated; personally, I have only a very rudimentary understanding of it, and I've never attempted to read the whole of the *Flower*.

Thanks, I'll take a look.

16th November 2007, 11:30 #7
TR: Junior Member
Re: The Secret of the Golden Flower
VERY interesting. So Tao is the air that separates into Yin and Yang (our two nostrils), creating these energies in our bodies. If we don't waste our seed, then it is made into light that will change our sperm yellow, and produce the elixir of life, giving us longer lives. I just read it quickly, but is this accurate?

16th November 2007, 02:12 PM #8
TR: Junior Member
Re: The Secret of the Golden Flower
I had a weird thought: What if our cardiovascular system is the bodhi tree, the upper part the trunk and limbs, and the lower part

of our diaphragm and blood vessels are the roots. That would situate the Buddha in our upper solar plexus. Is this farfetched because I have heard that we should contemplate our navel? - Or is that for a different reason? I am a religious theorist.

————————————————

17th November 2007, 04:15 AM #9

TK: Super Moderator

Re: The Secret of the Golden Flower

Quote: VERY interesting. So Tao is the air that separates into Yin and Yang (our two nostrils), creating these energies in our bodies. If we don't waste our seed, then it is made into light that will change our sperm yellow, and produce the elixir of life, giving us longer lives. I just read it quickly, but is this accurate?

Well, yes and no. Again, I am far from an expert on Chinese Alchemy, but there are at least some schools of thought that would regard this interpretation as overly crude and physical. Part of the problem is that there's no direct translation for many of the words being used, and so terms like "elixir" (*dan*, 丹) or "breath" (*qi* or *ch'i* 氣) often lose much of the meaning in translation.

To give an example, I believe the word being rendered as "sperm," for instance, is *jing* (精), one of the "Three Treasures" (*san bao* 三寶) of Daoism.

Although associated with seminal fluid, the term is actually far more encompassing and not necessarily a physical "substance," for instance it can also be equated with the psychological energy of eros or libido. Plus, more generally, it can refer to a state of bodily health or vitality. There's also the notion that *jing* as health is closely associated with a self-repeating pattern or process—a beautiful description of *jing* that I've heard is:

"Circulating in steady patterns, in channels, wearing a groove in time."

Furthermore, it is clear that *jing* is something inherited from one's parents and ancestors. As such, some TCM practitioners actually associate *jing* with DNA instead of with sperm per se.

Thomas Cleary, probably one of the most popular translators of Daoist texts, renders *jing* as "essence," which is succinct but really carries none of the connotations I've described above.

As you can see, it's a devil of a term to translate. The other two treasures of Daoism, *qi* (which Clearly renders as "energy") and *shen* (神, which Clearly renders as "spirit"), are even harder to pin down. The traditional Daoist method of cultivation speaks of refining *jing* into *qi*, *qi* into *shen*, *shen* into emptiness (*shu*).

17th November 2007, 04:31 AM #10

TK: Super Moderator

Re: The Secret of the Golden Flower

Quote: I had a weird thought: What if our cardiovascular system is the bodhi tree, the upper part the trunk and limbs, and the lower part of our diaphragm and blood vessels are the roots. That would situate the Buddha in our upper solar plexus. Is this farfetched because I have heard that we should contemplate our navel? - Or is that for a different reason? I am a religious theorist.

I'm not sure about Buddhism, but that's not too far from certain notions in Daoism and Chinese Alchemy.

In Daoist thought, the human being is considered a microcosm of the cosmos—in particular, "earth" or "the land" is closely associated with the body (hence the *Daodejing*, which is primarily a political text, is also indirectly about how to "rule" one's body as well as the state). In the context of Chinese alchemy, the body is envisioned like this:

That's supposed to be a rough outline of a person sitting. Toward the bottom, you'll notice the little "sun" with the four *taijitu* (or "yin-yang symbols"). This is the lower *dan tian*, a major focus point for internal cultivation and meditation. It's supposed to correspond with the individual's center of gravity, which is slightly below (and behind) the navel.

The lower *dan tian* is associated with *jing*, by the way, and the two others—located near the heart and the pituitary gland (or "third eye") respectively—are associated with *qi* and *shen*.

Unless I'm mistaken, this roughly corresponds with the Yogic idea of the chakras, although I believe in the various schools of Yoga there are more chakras marked than there are *dan tians* in the Daoist tradition.[2]

If the book's Secret Teachings are authentic, why have the book's many devotees been unable to explain these secrets? Why have the books written about the symbolic language and hidden meaning in *The Secret of the Golden Flower* not revealed the how-to functioning of the backward-flowing method?

It's not that the book's many readers missed something or that investigators didn't do their job; rather, it's that those readers and investigators didn't understand what the job entailed, didn't know what they should be looking for. Why do I say they didn't *know what they were looking for?*

These Secret Teachings cannot be unlocked by research. What do I mean by research? By research, I mean the modern scholastic techniques of translating and interpreting Chinese characters, of equating the Chinese symbols with notions of Western psychology and other disciplines, of cross-referencing symbols and meanings, of labeling and dating, of writing an interpretive analysis, of locating and reviewing secondary or tertiary sources. It cannot be made manifest by any doctorate level PH.D approach to understanding. Don't believe me? Google the book on Amazon. Both the Cleary and the Wilhelm versions. Take a look at the comments.[3] Reread the above chat room transcript. The writers are hung up on cross-cultural semantics and epistemology. No big deal; many have fallen into the same trap—even the hallowed Wilhelm/Baynes translation dances around the true meaning of the backward-flowing method. Read Richard Wilhelm's *A Discussion of the Text* in the Wilhelm/Baynes translation of *The Secret of the Golden Flower*. Although he mentions the backward-flowing method, at no time does he present a step-by-step description of how the backward-flowing method actually works. He seems content on explaining how he came up with the term *backward-flowing* from the German term *rücklaüfig*.

Outside of the *T'ai I Chin Hua Tsung Chih*[4] text itself, there is no commentary on, much less a how-to explanation of, the actual *backward-flowing method* process. In fact, at one point Carl Jung warns westerners, "In total misapprehension of all that I say in my commentary, such readers tried to imitate the 'method' described in the Chinese text." But what is the method? That's never explicitly dealt with, although the Wilhelm/Baynes translation does a better job of presenting the method in an instructional form than its Cleary counterpart.[5]

Why shouldn't a novice, or an adept for that matter, attempt to follow the method in the book, if indeed, it is a method? What's wrong with doing just that? Especially if we substitute the more appropriate word *practice* for Jung's ill-chosen figure of speech *imitate*. How do you imitate a method? You either do it or you don't. In fact, the only way of deciphering the secrets in the *Golden Flower* is by practicing the techniques in the book. Perhaps Jung was afraid that the reader might develop some sort of schizophrenic brainlock. Maybe the whole thing is a sinister ritual for turning practitioners into werewolves.

The only way to find out is to do it. And that's what I did. Perhaps I didn't realize the inherent dangers of attempting meditation without a guide. Perhaps it was sheer stubbornness. Nevertheless, the only way to find out was to do, especially since, as it turned out, I had to find a means of correcting a physical deformity. I was desperate, and desperation drives people to find solutions—one way or another.

> Things must be taken simply, not philosophically. Certainly, if we begin to think philosophically that there is no such thing as freedom [Life Force] then there is nothing left but to die.[6]

I don't think I'd be exaggerating if I said that most readers, who have picked up *The Secret of the Golden Flower*, whether they've read it entirely or only in part, have not practiced the method. No wonder, then, that no adequate step-by-step explanation of the backward-flowing method exists. As a consequence, *The Secret of the Golden Flower* has been regarded as a treatise on comparative literature or a trophy item for late night party talk.

In the end, deciphering *The Secret of the Golden Flower* is not so much a question of *what do the symbols mean*, as *how does the book's intrinsic method work*, for knowledge of the backward-flowing method comes only through empirical practice. In fact, there's no point in even discussing the meaning of the book's symbolic language. Suppose, for a moment, you actually knew the true meaning of every sentence and symbol. Besides a license for esoteric name dropping, what would this knowledge give you? Nothing. Nada. The method, as presented in the book, would still be difficult to follow because there is no sequential arrangement of the important techniques. You would still have to work your way through the method without any formal guidelines. And that's the point of this book: to fashion a clearly defined, unambiguous method where before there was none. That's what this book is: a handbook for those interested in the practice and the teaching of Golden Flower Meditation.

It is not the point of this present work to attempt a scholarly analysis of *The Secret of the Golden Flower*; rather, this book is meant to clarify how the backward-flowing method and the *Golden Flower*'s other techniques actually work, how they fit into the overall meditation model, what they will do for the individual who succeeds in mastering them, and how the backward-flowing method is really the crux of the Secret Teachings—*the Secret of Life*. In short, the only interpreting this book attempts is an explanation of the backward-flowing method drawn from a personal empirical application.

CRUISING AHEAD

If you can't hold back and must skip ahead to the Secret Teachings to learn about the backward-flowing method, go to *Chapter 4 – Hydraulics & Pneumatics*. When you're finished, I implore you to come back to this point in the text, for these teachings have little value unless placed in the overall Golden Flower context, so their relevance to the cosmology of life can be understood. Moreover, you will need this contextual understanding in order to appreciate how the techniques of the Secret Teachings go way beyond the realm of mere living, for practiced over a lifetime, these techniques ultimately develop a heightened sense of self-awareness, the very discipline needed to navigate through the afterlife state referred to in *The Tibetan Book of the Dead* as the *Between*.

Is There or Isn't There?

I am also an empiricist. To understand what is happening, you have to work as a synoptic empiricist, and you must have the experience. You must pray, or meditate, and when you have these experiences, it is overwhelmingly apparent. There is no doubt these domains exist.

~ *The Future of the Body* — Michael Murphy,
Esalen Institute

Do the Secret Teachings really exist? Is there a Secret to Life? Some sort of trick, magic spell, or elixir, a technique capable of triggering rejuvenation and extraordinary powers?

If it exists, is it freely available to anyone? Or only a select few? Is it hidden in plain sight, or concealed behind riddles and enigmas? Or like the Freemasons, does it require admission and initiation into some secret group?

Could it be something we eat? Something we do? Something someone gives us, teaches us, or shows us how to use? Something we have to accomplish, like a quest? Perhaps, it's a substance, the magic H^2O sought by Ponce de Leon from the Fountain of Youth? Perhaps it entails manipulation of elements *à la* medieval alchemy?

What makes it tick? How do we apply it? What capabilities would it have to bestow on us in order to qualify as the *one and only* true Secret of Life? Is it an operation to be performed? A magic spell? A trick? The result of an interplanetary visitation or transmission?

Perhaps it's based on love or faith, or some other abstraction. Perhaps it's simply prayer.

What is it? Where do we find it? How do we know when we've found it? What will it do for us? Will it work the same way for each individual?

Throughout history, the subject has been raised many times, taken on many forms, had many advocates, been the object of many claims. This or that tonic, such and such magic charm, the true faith, eternal life; transforming lead into gold, the Word becoming Flesh.

We've heard the claims and listened to the legends. Yet, after all that has been said and done, we remain, at best, doubtful, more likely indifferent or confused.

We ask: Does it really exist? Is there really a Secret to Life? And rightfully so. Its essence has infused our culture. Yet, there is no one, all-encompassing truth, only a yearning for something more powerful, more liberating. For instance, since the 1940s, Hollywood has featured movies in which people:

- Come back from the dead to instruct the living (*Ghost, Heaven Can Wait*);
- Have guardian angels (*It's a Wonderful Life, Topper, Here Comes Mr. Jordan, The Bishop's Wife*);
- Learn to use secret powers (*Star Wars, Superman, The Matrix*).

If they do it in the movies, if it's seeped into our consciousness to such an extent, surely there must be something to it. Doesn't fiction usually foretell reality? Is not actuality rooted in dreams? If there's nothing to it, then why has so much time and money been spent stimulating our imagination?

> And now, a swell kicker: Zen is also the name of a new booze product, a liqueur, something allegedly flavored to taste like green tea and ready to mix with your fave vodka or sake, or whatever the hell you can think of, because nothing says 'deeply calming ancient spiritual practice' like, you know, knocking back shots of artificially sweetened moss-green liquid containing 20 percent alcohol by volume. Mmm, nurturing.
>
> Actually, I sort of love the silly audacity of it. You almost have to. I mean, isn't it just the cutest thing, the warped and shameless co-opting of all things divine and succorific to a crazed populace starved for meaning and sustenance in every purchase and in every desire and in every vice, and never really finding it? It so absolutely is.[7]

So, why do we spend so much time on stories and fables about the acquisition of extraordinary faculties? Quite simply, because there's a large body of experience in fact and fiction built up around the acquisition of such faculties.

We shouldn't be indignant with Hollywood. The purveyors of dreams—pop culture trendsetters and advertising wags, writers and storytellers—are merely channeling the phenomenon of *unconscious* or *collective yearning*. What is *unconscious yearning*?

Episodes of collective *unconscious yearning* usually precede periods of actualization, moments in history when the rubber meets the road—the times when fantastical ideas begin to bear fruit. For example, discoveries in the field of bacteriology by men like Ferdinand Cohn (1828–1898), Louis Pasteur (1822–1895), and Robert Koch (1843–1910) occurred about the same time in history and were preceded by social and technological changes that helped cultivate an awareness of the underlying issues. When the leading figures appeared on the scene, there *preexisted* a climate of acceptance. Not absolute acceptance, of course. No, innovators usually have to beat back skepticism. Nevertheless, it's hard to imagine this particular breakthrough (micro-bacteriological discoveries) taking place at the time of, say, the Egyptian pharaohs.

All movements need fertile soil to grow in. And that soil is the collective *unconscious yearning* of a culture, a particular conjunction of circumstances and timing. This phenomenon is related to Bucke's *Cosmic Consciousness*, a condition cited in William James' *The Varieties of Religious Experience*:

> In its more striking instances [Cosmic Consciousness] is not simply an extension or an expansion of the self-conscious mind with which we are all familiar, but the superaddition of a function as distinct from any possessed by the average man as self-consciousness is distinct from any function possessed by the higher animals.[8]

Cosmic Consciousness specifies a qualitative *leap* in consciousness. In his 1968 masterpiece, *2001: A Space Odyssey*, Stanley Kubrick represents this leap by the sudden appearance of a monolith in the midst of primitive tribes people. One individual picks up a bone and suddenly realizes that it can be used as a weapon. The viewer understands that these primitives have become aware of *self and other* (self-consciousness) and will henceforth be able to create and use tools. Kubrick's symbolization of the last great leap in consciousness didn't include a backstory for the opposing tribe that gets slaughtered during the ensuing skirmish. We are left thinking that it will soon be over for them, that the tribe who has learned to use weapons will have a technological advantage for a long time.

But this doesn't coincide very well with what we know about technology: Knowledge fans out horizontally at an alarming rate. People learn and adapt; they reverse engineer, find resourceful ways to level the playing field. *Unconscious yearning* represents the desire to make up for lost ground, to compete at a higher level. It's more about the way ideas, tendencies, and faculties spread than about the ideas, tendencies, and faculties themselves.

Another example of *unconscious yearning*: the Enlightenment in France and England. Rousseau, Voltaire, and their precursors: Descartes, Bacon, and Hobbes; Locke, Hume, etc.; men who appeared at the exact moment their contributions would create maximum impact on the culture—a culture that was primed to receive it.

How does this theory apply to the Secret Teachings? Well, quite simply our present age is the culmination of *unconscious yearning* episodes focused on the Secret of Life and other so-called New Age issues. At first, the whole New Age thing might seem like escapism, but it's not. Just because Hollywood has mastered special effects that defy gravity and has popularized *The Force* doesn't mean movies featuring secret powers aren't the result of *unconscious yearning* or the residue of lost teachings. It's a movement whose time has come. Numinous though it may be, it has entered the here and now of our age.

Am I making a prediction? No, predictions are dangerous; they smack of fundamentalist claptrap (end times and rapture). I'm merely stating facts and drawing probable conclusions:

1) The Secret of Life has always existed in the form of a latent energy source [the Life Force] within each individual.

2) The Secret Teachings—the practical knowledge of the Kundalini meditation techniques for activating the Life Force—have been restricted to a limited few, who have usually insisted that God (or his inner circle) wanted it this way.

3) Periodic attempts have been made to vulgarize these secrets.

4) These attempts have failed, or the teachings were deemed subversive or heretical and were suppressed.

5) We now have instant access. Communications (Internet, worldwide press, and television) and transportation (air

travel and superhighways). Instant access has rekindled interest in the Secret of Life. Ergo, it is reasonable to believe that the planetary buzz around the Secret of Life could eventually lead to a serious investigation.

Unlike the periods of *unconscious yearning* that led to the Enlightenment, the *unconscious yearning* that surrounds the Secret of Life stretches over many centuries. Yet, only recently has it culminated, because, until recently, the whole question of the Secret of Life has been subdivided and fragmented. It's existed as an outcropping of religion and mysticism. It's been the focus of esoteric science, such as alchemy—part and parcel of myths such as Ponce de Leon's Fountain of Youth. It's been opposed by organized religions that want to maintain their monopoly on God's grace and salvation. It's been beaten down by Cartesian philosophers, only to rise again under the banner of those seeking a connection between science and metaphysics: pragmatists like Michael Talbot popularizing the relation between space-time and cosmic consciousness, physicists like David Bohm writing on quantum theory and consciousness, empiricists like Gopi Krishna inviting the scientific vetting of the Kundalini awakening process. But think about how hard it is to complete the process. Think about the odds of doing so.

To put the following flowchart in perspective, imagine a similar chart tracing the path of a typical American doctorate level education. The process is long—getting a PhD is a grueling process—but the information is readily available. Want to study chemistry? No problem. Ten thousand college catalogues at your disposal. Get good grades in high school, find a college that suits you and you're on your way. On the other hand, informing yourself about the Secret Teachings is not so easy. There is no approved curriculum, no regulating body, no accepted practices, no *Secret Teachings for Dummies* guidebooks. You're on your own. All you have is your own inspired motivation, some hint that there may be something out there—something that fascinates you. But beyond that you have no idea what's in store for you.

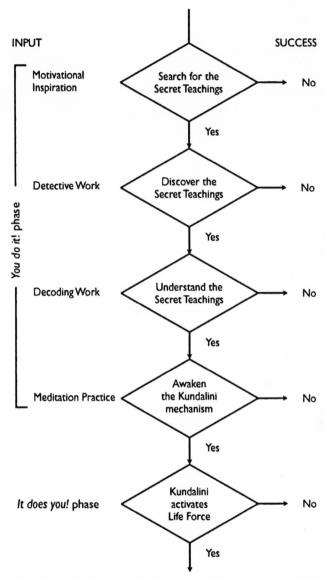

Figure 1: Flowchart of the Life Force activation process—from inspiration to completion.

The Secret of Life—from the initial search-for-truth stage to the final activation of the Life Force stage—should not be thought of as a single event, but a flow of events, each one with a slim likelihood of completion. So much goes into completing the process: inspiration, discovery, detective work, exercise, meditation—to say nothing of frustration, disappointment, and disinformation. The path is long, hard, and uncertain, because up till now, no one permanent, voluntary, safe, repeatable method existed for shepherding a novice through the entire process.

On the chart you will notice there are two phases, what Ram Dass called the *You do it!* and *It does you!* phases. In the first phase, you do all the work. You find the requisite inspiration, be it conscious or unconscious, deliberate or accidental. Whatever! It's up to you to find it. The detective work, the decoding, the practice are also up to you. It's only during the last phase that things get really interesting. Not that they're uninteresting beforehand. But there definitely is a reward phase when *It* does *You*. Your job is to make your way through the obstacles to this phase.

Until recently, there has been no way to assemble and examine all sides of the Secret of Life issue, no way of defining its limits, its capabilities. No way of proving its existence. That time is here, but it hasn't always been that way.

Consider the fact that in the 14th Century, Ibn Khatima and Ibn al-Khatib wrote of infectious diseases being caused by contagious entities that entered the human body. These ideas, about the contagious nature of diseases, remained unexplored in Europe and did not surface again until the Renaissance, when in 1676, Anton van Leeuwenhoek, using a microscope of his own design, prepared the way for Pasteur and his cohorts. Then, of course, it took many years for the discoveries of Pasteur to reach the rest of the world. Now, we have instant recognition, instant access. Compartmentalization of information is a thing of the past, or should be.

Kids in China play with plastic light sabers just like kids in America. But do they know what the point of the game is? Why, it's *The Force*, of course—the Life Force—the Secret of Life.

Hollywood wants to sell us tickets. The pharmaceutical industry wants us to believe we can squeeze it out of a tube. Agrobusiness tells us we can take off the pounds while adding years to our lives. Doctors, let's not forget doctors, advertise sure-fire cures and interventions certain to make us feel good about ourselves.

Everyone wants it; it should be a bonanza. So, why is everyone feeling so lost?

Suicide rates are climbing, mental illness and depression are running rampant, diabetes has risen to epidemic proportions, drug abuse and alcoholism are heading through the roof, sexual addiction is pandemic. At the same time, cosmetic sales are up; organic foods have taken off; healthy lifestyles are gaining; Yoga is on the cover of *Time*.

The time is right; it is also rife. In the near future, people will demand more from meditation; they won't settle for stress reduction and relaxation. This shouldn't upset us; change is normal. Over time, every system adds features and sophistication. Meditation is no different. The backward-flowing method transforms the basic meditation of today into a second generation system for unlocking Kundalini in a safe, permanent fashion that produces a wealth of metanormal effects and, as a result, a palpable change in being. By identifying the true secrets of Life and Death and explaining how they work, this book opens up new horizons for pioneering Yoga and meditation teachers and students.

While alive, we tend to think of Life and Death as linked in a morally causative fashion: The good and bad deeds we do during our lifetimes influence our stature in the afterlife. Certainly, in the West, we do not imagine that by discovering a technique for self-improvement in one stage, we might carry it over and use it in the next stage—the stages being the endless cycle of birth, life, death, rebirth. But what if Life and Death are inextricably linked in exactly that way? What if certain techniques could be acquired in one stage and used in the next? In order to answer these questions, we must first learn the Secret of Life. However, before we do that, we must first explore the methodologies used to validate the Secret Teachings.

FIRSTHAND OR SECONDHAND?

There is no question of faith or belief in all this. Quite the opposite, this system teaches people to believe in absolutely nothing. You must verify everything that you see, hear, or feel. Only in that way can you come to something.

~ *The Fourth Way* – P.D. Ouspensky

I THINK, THEREFORE I AM.

Sounds logical, even comforting, a worthy tribute to that matchless organ, the human brain. Its evolutionary potential is unlimited. It's as if we only need to sit back, secure in the knowledge that in a dualistic world, the human brain is the master of all it surveys. In the future, rooms full of highly-evolved gray matter will toil away on our behalf. Row after row of vats filled with nourishing broth, each one containing a brain, linked by cables to computers that control all communications, operate all machinery and make all our decisions. All we have to do is play golf.

> Though we can conceive such progress in [an] economical manner, I am led by data, such as those presented in this book, to believe that the self-evident break with normal consciousness and behavior, the transcendence of certain needs, and the self-mastery of mind and flesh characteristic of metanormal functioning would, if realized by enough people, create a new kind of life on this planet.[9]

The logical extension of the perfection of our intelligence: bodiless brains, bionic tissue at the service of mankind. The science fiction result of the Rationalist vision. I think, therefore the world is. Not because it really is, but because the brain says it is. If it weren't for the all-knowing brain, the world wouldn't be there.

And sooner than we imagine, it just might not be. For in spite of our creativity, we are close to collapse.

We've done such a good job of building and creating, classifying and controlling, we've lost sight of the destruction we've caused. Perhaps the famous Cartesian maxim needs to be revised: "I think, therefore I destroy."

Animals could do a better job preserving the planet. If the Animal Kingdom ruled the world, we'd still have tropical rainforests, clear skies, honeybees, and clean water. No polluted rivers, no Bermuda Triangle of floating plastic debris, no planetary drought, no global apocalypse, no food shortages, no war.

I'm not diatribing. I am merely pointing out that what we think is progress really does have other implications. The brain is a great tool. So, why do we use it only to move forward? Why can't we use it to explore the byways, the hidden dimensions of life? Say, from back to front, from end to beginning, from effect to cause. Let's start with some assumptions about what the real Secret of Life ought to do for us. Let's take a look at the results and work our way back to the cause. Here are my criteria for the Secret of Life. It must be able to:

- Trigger autonomic self-healing mechanisms capable of correcting defects related to neural degeneration;
- Allow me to overcome all addictions;
- Reverse any self-destructive behavior, allow me greater emotional control;
- Rejuvenate my body as it ages, keeping it at least 10 years younger than its actual chronological age;
- Heighten and enhance my consciousness by triggering various metanormal effects and powers;
- Refine my being to the point where I am able to effect a release from Karmic bondage;
- Show me that the ego persists after death and provide me with the tools to face death;
- Facilitate the transition into the next state of being.

Sure, there are many other amazing faculties that I could add to this list: the ability to fly, to pass through walls, to heal the sick…but let's stick with the basics for the moment, for we need to understand why these effects of the Secret of Life take precedence over all other effects.

In the next chapter, I will reveal the Secret of Life and Death. I will describe how it works, the process of activating it, how to avail oneself of its power, what its properties actually consist of, and what they will do for you. I will also explain how it fits into the cosmology of life. At the same time, I will describe how, within this governing cosmology, the brain is not—I repeat *not*—the leading system in our bodies. It is only one of many subsystems in our holistic organism. I will explain how the principle referred to in *The Secret of the Golden Flower* as the *Primal Spirit*— the venerable text's term for the Life Force—is really the dominant system of the body. Our brains would not exist without it. For the moment, however, I want to explore the methodology used to master the secret teachings of the Golden Flower. To accomplish this, we must have some understanding of how people—you and I, scholars and researchers—*know what we know* or *know what we think we know*. The following citation presents a discussion of two rival philosophical approaches; it is a good place to start.

> The dispute between rationalism and empiricism concerns the extent to which we are dependent upon sense experience in our effort to gain knowledge. Rationalists claim that there are significant ways in which our concepts and knowledge are gained independently of sense experience. Empiricists claim that sense experience is the ultimate source of all our concepts and knowledge.
>
> Rationalists generally develop their view in two ways. First, they argue that there are cases where the content of our concepts or knowledge outstrips the information that sense experience can provide. Second, they construct accounts of how reason in some form or other provides that additional information about the world. Empiricists present complementary lines of thought. First, they develop accounts of how experience provides the information that rationalists cite, insofar as we have it in the first place. (Empiricists will at times opt for skepticism as an alternative to rationalism: if experience cannot provide the concepts or knowledge the rationalists cite, then we don't have them.) Second, empiricists attack the rationalists' accounts of how reason is a source of concepts or knowledge.[10]

I don't want this to devolve into an epistemological debate, nor do I want to plug one side or put down the other. To master any subject, both observational skills and the ability to reason are needed. However, it is important to understand that in the attempt to unravel the truth about the Secret Teachings, certain knowledge adds very little to the discussion. In fact, the more one examines the knowledge on the subject, the more one realizes that most of it serves no purpose. Sadly, this is due to the way this so-called knowledge came into being.

I say *sadly* because most so-called knowledge is not knowledge, but information. There is a difference. Information is just out there, undifferentiated bits of jetsam. Is it true or false?

Most of the time, we don't really know or care. We don't have the time to verify it. Knowledge, on the other hand, is derived from reliable data, which can be, and is shaped into theories to explain the big picture. Knowledge is useful. We can't be certain that a theory or process will hold up over time, but it is reliable as long as the data is.

Suppose I come across a document written in an unknown language. I take it to an expert. He tells me it's written in a combination of Pahlavi and Arabic. He tells me that although slightly ambiguous, the Pahlavi section of the manuscript appears to describe a device, which the Arabic section translates roughly as *flux capacitor*. The Arabic section implies that the *flux capacitor* is a device for generating inexhaustible energy. The Arabic section goes on to provide information about the political situation at the time of the discovery, the assassination of the ruler who championed the development of the device, and a plague, which occurred at the moment of his death. As more experts pour over the document, arguments arise about the meaning of the Pahlavi section. Most experts believe the symbolic language is too vague to be of any material value; only a few believe that the *flux capacitor* was ever an actual working device. They believe it represents a symbolic expression of the beliefs of a heretic sect of Zoroastrian priests.

Nevertheless, over time many books are written about the document, including some that use other sources to expand on the circumstances around the ruler's death. Namely, that it occurred in 666 BC, that it took place at longitude 66° / latitude 33° during the lunar eclipse of October 15, 0666. Investigators become obsessed with the numerological significance of the dates and numbers. Backed by dubious computations, they put together various theses proving that the ruler will reappear on a given date sometime in the future. These theses give way to others. Soon, there is no mention of the root issue—the *flux capacitor*, the device to generate unlimited free energy. All has been subverted in a self-indulgent race to prove that each succeeding researcher is more knowledgeable on the subject of numerology, more capable of explaining the significance of a few coincidences. Finally, all is derivative jetsam. No one ever bothers to decipher the plans and build a prototype device.

Sound familiar? I call it *tripping on coincidence*: one thing leading to another without any data to support it; secondhand associations fabricated from a series of coincidences. Here's a more up-to-date example:

> LANDOVER, Md. — The Washington Redskins were drenched with rain, sweat and even a few cathartic tears Sunday evening when they entered their locker room after a 27-6 demolition of the Dallas Cowboys. Rock Cartwright screamed: "We won by 21! We won by 21!" Several teammates joined in, the chants growing louder and louder, until the refrain echoed off the walls.
>
> "No one had to explain anything," defensive end Chris Wilson said. "We all knew what he was talking about."
>
> On a day when they capped an unlikely late-season surge by clinching the National Football Conference's final playoff berth, that the Redskins' margin of victory matched the jersey number worn by Sean Taylor, the promising safety who was shot to death last month, was a delicious coincidence to only those who have not been paying attention to what has happened over the last month.[11]

All well and good. I'm glad that the Redskins won, happy that they won by 21. But besides providing a great lead-in for SPORTS CENTER, does it prove anything? Sure, it's not sinister in and of itself, but one has to question an associative technique that has become an accepted methodology for many people.

THE SECRET TEACHINGS & CHRISTIANITY

When you think about it, a lot of historical research is based on flawed associations, opinion, spin, and public relations. Take the Bible, for instance. Few of Jesus' original firsthand teachings have survived. We don't really know what Jesus said. In fact, we can't be sure that various "authorities" didn't spin, modify, or suppress His teachings to meet their own ends—and not just in recent times to suit the ends of politically-motivated TV evangelists and fundamentalist talk show hosts, but from the first century onward. When you think about it, we don't know very much about His life, not in its entirety. For example, some researchers have discovered source materials that say He was not only influenced by, but actually visited, the Orient and studied Eastern mysticism. According to the Himi manuscript discovered in a Ladakh monastery in 1887:

> At the age of thirteen, [Jesus] set out toward Sind (a region in present-day southeast Pakistan in the lower Hindus River valley) with 'the object of perfecting himself in the Divine Word and of studying the laws of the great Buddhas.'
>
> He spent six years in Nepal, according to the text. He mastered the Pali language and became 'a perfect expositor of the sacred writings' of Buddhism. Sometime between the ages of twenty-seven and twenty-nine, he left the Himalayas and journeyed west, preaching along the way.[12]

The point of this is not to go off subject, but to underline that although the Secret Teachings were known to many religions, they became the basis of only a few, even though, in the case of Christianity, there are many documents that support both the story of Jesus' traveling to the East to cultivate and expand His knowledge of the Secret Teachings, and the accounts that they were part of His ministry. Let's assume that these accounts are true. Then why are the Secret Teachings no longer part of the Christian faith? Modern investigators tell us they were at the beginning, but that a controversy arose over the subject of whether the Secret Teachings should be included in church doctrines.

Named after Arius, a 3rd century monk, the Arian Controversy caused a major schism in Christianity. According to the Arians, the Secret Teachings opened the way to perfection for each and every individual. On the other hand, the orthodox Christians, the opponents of Arius, believed that the Secret Teachings disputed the idea of Jesus' divinity.

> The Arians claimed that Jesus became God's Son and therefore demonstrated a universal principle that all beings can follow. But the orthodox said that he had always been God's Son, was of the same essence as God (and therefore was God) and could not be imitated by mere creatures, who lack God's essence. Salvation could come only by accessing God's grace via the Church.[13]

According to the orthodox faction, baptism in the church provided the only means to salvation; there was no spiritual "deliverance" outside the church. In essence, because God's grace was the only means to heaven, this made the representatives of the church the gatekeepers to salvation. The Christian mystics, Arians and Gnostics, on the other hand, believed in reincarnation and the *practice* of merging with the Creator—the Creative Life Force—or *Nirvana*, as the Buddhists called it. They believed that over time a man could perfect himself. They believed Jesus was more like Buddha, a highly-developed being who had *perfected* himself. Notice that I stressed the word *practice* above. The Secret Teachings are all about *practicing* techniques, not about arguing theology or professing faith.

Reincarnation: The Missing Link in Christianity by Elizabeth Clare Prophet explains this controversy in detail, and how, over the course of many years, the orthodox group won out. Now, let's suppose the research in her book accurately portrays the ways in which the Secret Teachings were once part of Christianity before being systematically exorcized. If so, it provides us with a stark contrast between Eastern and Western religions. The Secret Teachings have survived in the Eastern religions and have been passed down to us in the form of *meditational* practice and techniques, the highest and most complete of which is the *backward-flowing method*. The Western religions are about believing in events, most of which cannot be verified historically, and having faith in what the church tells you about the nature of God and His Son. The point of many Eastern religions is for each individual to discover and use the Secret Teachings to perfect himself over many lifetimes, if necessary, or over one, like Jesus and Buddha did. The Secret Teachings lay down the roadmap to perfection; techniques like the backward-flowing method are the means to this end.

It's easy to see why the Arian precepts got lost in the shuffle. The Arian Controversy happened a long time ago; only a few dedicated scholars still deliberate over it. As a result, we accept the orthodox version of events and their doctrinal teachings as official and we "learn" the orthodox doctrines by rote. As a young man growing up in the Episcopal Church, I repeated the Apostles' Creed along with everyone else, without understanding what I was actually saying. What's so bad about that? you wonder. Well, it's not bad if you truly understand what you're saying and you do so because you agree with each and every word. But do you? I didn't, and only found out about it recently.

APOSTLES' CREED

I believe in God, the Father Almighty,
    the Creator of heaven and earth,
    and in Jesus Christ, His only Son, our Lord:
Who was conceived of the Holy Spirit,
    born of the Virgin Mary,
    suffered under Pontius Pilate,
    was crucified, died, and was buried.
He descended into hell
The third day He arose again from the dead.
He ascended into heaven
    and sits at the right hand of God the Father Almighty,
    whence He shall come to judge the living and the dead.
I believe in the Holy Spirit, the holy Catholic Church,
    the communion of saints,
    the forgiveness of sins,
    the resurrection of the body,
    and life everlasting.
Amen.

THE NICENE CREED

I believe in one God, the Father Almighty, Maker of heaven and earth, and of all things visible and invisible.

And in one Lord Jesus Christ, the only-begotten Son of God, begotten of the Father before all worlds; God of God, Light of Light, very God of very God; begotten, not made, being of one substance with the Father, by whom all things were made.

Who, for us men and for our salvation, came down from heaven, and was incarnate by the Holy Spirit of the virgin Mary, and was made man; and was crucified also for us under Pontius Pilate; He suffered and was buried; and the third day He rose again, according to the Scriptures; and ascended into heaven, and sits on the right hand of the Father; and He shall come again, with glory, to judge the quick and the dead; whose kingdom shall have no end.

And I believe in the Holy Ghost, the Lord and Giver of Life; who proceeds from the Father and the Son; who with the Father and the Son together is worshipped and glorified; who spoke by the prophets.

And I believe one holy Catholic and Apostolic Church. I acknowledge one baptism for the remission of sins; and I look for the resurrection of the dead, and the life of the world to come. Amen.

These two Creeds were produced as a reaction to the Arian Controversy. As a young boy I repeated the Apostles' Creed without realizing that "the resurrection of the body" meant reassembling the physical body in heaven.

I had no empirical way of determining the validity of these statements, so I just repeated them. A classic example of *not knowing what you think you know.* Now after many years of practicing the Secret Teachings, I can say that not only do I not believe that the physical body gets reassembled in Heaven, I have formulated an empirically derived thesis based on my meditation practice that validates the Arian interpretation of Jesus' mission and teachings, the same teachings that are the basis of Taoism and Buddhism.

To understand this thesis, let's look at a contrasting example of "spiritual" research, one based on the empirical data I observed during a meditation practice that led to the activation of the Life Force, a practice I used to formulate and test this theory. In a previous book, *Deciphering the Golden Flower One Secret at a Time*, I put forth a theory that a sentient agent intervenes at the split-second moment before conception to design a unique blueprint for individual substantiation. This is the type of empirical approach Gopi Krishna urged me to pursue, using, as he said, the Secret Teachings to provide "indisputable evidence for the existence of design in creation."

We are all perfect at that split-second moment before conception. Of course, like a building before the foundation is laid, at that moment our beings are only blueprints. These blueprints—the numinous plans laid out for our substantiation—are perfect. At the moment of conception—the moment the egg is fertilized by the sperm—the body begins to take shape. It's the moment when, were we able to stand over our perfect blueprints, we might wonder if they can be executed as designed. That's the job of the Life Force. The Life Force has many names: Kundalini, sublimation, Tantra, alchemy, serpent power, primordial energy, cosmic power, Qi, Reiki, and Primal Spirit. Until the moment of birth, the Life Force controls our substantiation. The moment we are born we become conscious and our natural life force becomes inactive. After we're born, something always seems to interfere with our continued growth. We get sick, accidents occur, we become addicted, we grow older, our bodies break down. It's not that things can't happen while we are in the womb, they can. By and large, however, our time in the womb is peaceful. But after we are born, the frequency of interference increases, because that's when we start doing things to ourselves. That's when we bring our will, or lack of it, to bear. That's when the serious damage is done.[14]

I now realize that my conclusions went beyond the thrust of the data available to me at the time. Recently, I became aware of a hypothesis based on genetic theory, which states that although there is indeed a unique blueprint for individual substantiation, it is the result of "natural selection acting on inherited traits" and it occurs during the reproduction process.

Darwin was convinced that species evolve over time—through natural selection acting on inherited traits. But he had no idea how those traits arose—or how they were passed from generation to generation.

When 20ᵗʰ century scientists discovered the role DNA plays in heredity, they founded a new science called genetics—that put Darwin's theory to the test. Virtually every cell in every living thing contains chromosomes—which are made of densely packed strands of DNA that function as a blueprint of the individual organism's characteristics.

During reproduction, chromosomes from each parent replicate and shuffle their parts to produce new chromosomes. Then, each parent passes one chromosome to offspring. But the process is imperfect. Along the way, DNA is subject to random mutations—or mistakes— which give each offspring its own unique blueprint.

Sometimes this produces characteristics in offspring that are benign. Other times it produces harmful characteristics—like a misshapen wing (in a butterfly). But occasionally, the process gives rise to a beneficial trait—for example, a butterfly whose coloration mimics another species that tastes bad to birds.[15]

My theory, the one proposed in my book *Deciphering the Golden Flower One Secret at a Time*, was based on the following data observed during and subsequent to my 1973 Kundalini-Life Force activation experience. Using the meditation method in *The Secret of the Golden Flower*, I activated the Life Force. Since I had no knowledge of the symbolic meaning of the text, I had to forge ahead bit by bit, learning each technique one at a time. This was a linear, empirical process, punctuated by a rational process that allowed me to connect the dots in certain instances. Only after mastering a particular technique did I realize what I needed to do next. When the Life Force activation process had finished, I was able to document the following:

- I observed the original blueprint for my unique bodily substantiation. In fact, after activating the Life Force, the blueprint lay over my actual physical body like a template shroud. At the same time, I could see it as if I was watching a three-dimensional computer graphic that I could turn and/or rotate at will around various axes.
- Over a period of months and years, I watched the Life Force stretch my physical body in all directions towards the boundaries of the blueprint. Eventually, I realized that my actual physical body had become deformed as a result of a childhood accident.[16] Every day, as I lay in meditation, a tremendous Life Force energy stretched my body outwards toward the blueprint outline that surrounded it, and every time I finished meditating, my body had expanded slightly.
- This process continued for thirty years, until my physical body corresponded perfectly with the blueprint.
- During the time that my body was expanding, I observed the Life Force using various resources, namely, the magic elixir of life (mentioned in *The Secret of the Golden Flower*),

involuntary movements (described in *The Secrets of Chinese Meditation* by Charles Luk), and a healing wind[17] (a resource not previously documented to my knowledge, which consists of the walls of the solar plexus parting and a force field of invisible—except to myself—energy shooting forth from the solar plexus, traveling outside the body in an arc-like trajectory to the third eye, which then opens like a castanet to receive it and spray it on the brain).

After observing these effects, I inferred that this blueprint had to have been saved in some ethereal, computer memory-like storage in order for it to be able to reappear at the moment the Life Force was activated. Where this blueprint had been stored between the time of my conception and my 35th year, I did not know. Material scientists, geneticists, in this instance, would probably say it resided in the brain, and that is a safe assumption, for it is unlikely that it resided outside the body. Nevertheless, the fact that I saw it and watched the Life Force energy use it to "reengineer" my body made me think that some sentient agency must play a role in reproduction, and in the design and formation of the body. Why had this blueprint suddenly appeared? Where had it been for thirty-five years? If it had no purpose, wouldn't it have ceased to exist? So then, it must have a purpose, for it was still there.

In any case, these observations were the reasons I decided that an independent sentient agent had created my blueprint, and I equated this as support for Intelligent Design, a deduction on my part that I now feel was premature.

Now that I know genetic theory specifies that reproduction involves random recombining of DNA in the creation of a unique individual blueprint, I accept that an individual's blueprint is not created at the split-second moment prior to conception, but that its creation takes place at the time of, and is part of, the process of reproduction. However, although genetic theory has added to the data I now have available, and has made me rethink my available data, I still am unable to completely reject the notion that a creative sentient agent intercedes during the DNA combining process.

I am not alone in concluding that sentience plays a role in reproduction:

The mediation-transcending—indeed, domain-transcending—growth of these various abilities constitutes a dramatic progress. Such advance suggests that evolution is influenced by purposes or agencies that to some extent subsume the mechanisms presently described by mainstream science. It invites us to wonder whether nature has a *telos*, or creative tendency, to manifest the activities I've labeled metanormal, a drive or attraction toward greater ends that appropriates the processes of any domain to produce more developed capacities. Paraphrasing a statement made by physicist Joseph Ford, if randomness evident in all evolution to date is characterized as a kind of dice-rolling, the extraordinary advances described here suggest that the dice are loaded.[18]

I have a sneaking suspicion, but will hold out until more data becomes available. What I am sure of—because I witnessed it—is that the Life Force is *activateable*. It can correct the deformity of those born with a perfect blueprint, that is, those individuals who have suffered from injury or malformation subsequent to birth.

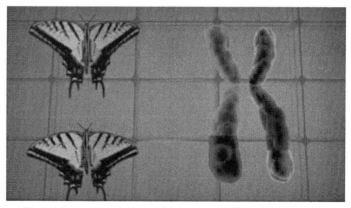

Figure 2: Each parent passes one chromosome to offspring.

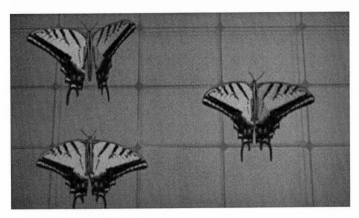

Figure 3: Normal offspring.

But what about an individual who was bequeathed an imperfect blueprint, an individual whose DNA became corrupted during the reproduction process? A butterfly with a misshapen wing? If the Life Force could correct the somatic and structural defects resulting from an imperfect DNA blueprint, wouldn't it prove that some sentient agency played a hand in the creation of the blueprint, that the blueprint came into existence before the moment of procreation? Now, proving that the Life Force could correct misalignment and malformation would entail a person with an imperfect DNA blueprint—an individual born with a defect—using restorative Golden Flower Meditation to activate the Life Force. If the Life Force proved capable of reengineering the person's body to correct an inherited defect or other "harmful characteristic," it would prove that a sentient agency played a role in constituting the blueprint in the first place, because the Life Force was able to go back to a time before the condition (inherited defect or other "harmful characteristic") was created, summon the blueprint that existed prior to conception from a memory source, correct the imperfections in the blueprint (by the laws of genetics, the blueprint must reflect those imperfections), and finally, correct the condition.

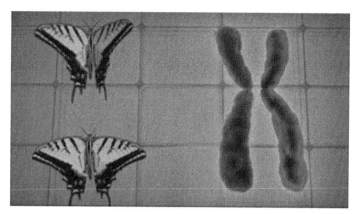

Figure 4: Harmful characteristics.

Practically, this would mean someone with a condition created during the conception process volunteering to practice restorative Golden Flower Meditation, using the backward–flowing method to activate the Life Force, which, in turn, would correct the defect.

Figure 5: Offspring resulting from harmful characteristics.

In order to investigate this postulate further, in the chapters ahead, we will examine the reproduction process through information presented in *The Tibetan Book of the Dead*. We will see how the transition from death to rebirth sheds light on my proposed experiment and how, should you decide to undertake this work, you will *know what you know.*

HYDRAULICS & PNEUMATICS

All meditatively valid subjective experiences must be verifiable by the same practitioner and through other individuals being able to attain the same state by the same practice. If they are thus verified, such states may be taken to be universal.

- *The Universe in a Single Atom* – The Dalai Lama

The goal of restorative Golden Flower Meditation (GFM) is to standardize the outcome of the Life Force activation process, in other words, to make the results of one meditation experience indistinguishable from the next. Why is this important? In his book, *The Future of the Body*, Michael Murphy performs an exhaustive study of what he calls metanormal experience or development. He catalogues his findings in twelve categories (I list ten of them below) under the heading of the "metanormalities of everyday life":

- Perception of Eternal Events
- Somatic Awareness and Self-Regulation
- Communication Abilities
- Vitality
- Movement Abilities
- Cognition
- Volition
- Individuation and Sense of Self
- Love
- Bodily Structures, States, and Processes

Here are a few examples of metanormal effects that I have experienced personally:

- Perception of External Events
  - Feeling that someone is watching you, after which you turn to meet his or her gaze.
  - Correctly sensing the location of lost objects without the help of sensory cues.
  - Opening books to the exact passage you are looking for.
  - Watching someone's face reveal—as if in slow motion—unsuspected feelings, traits, or possibilities for development.
  - Seeing lights around people or inanimate objects for which there are no apparent sources.
  - Looking at something familiar and seeing it as if for the first time.

- Somatic Awareness and Self-Regulation
  - Experiencing vivid images of arteries, capillaries, or other bodily structures that immediately seem to be your own, and sensing they may be damaged or in the process of recovery from injury.
  - Determining by spontaneous tastes or smells your level of stress during extreme exertion.
  - Picturing what appears to be charkas or other entities depicted in esoteric teachings.
- Communication Abilities
  - Saying something unexpected in unison with someone else.
  - Feeling no separation at all from your lover during sexual intercourse.
- Vitality
  - Sensing a rush of electricity up the spine or radiating out from the abdomen, accompanied by mental illuminations or great strength.
  - Remaining free of infection in spite of contagious diseases among those around you.
- Movement Abilities
  - Experiencing flight as if in a subtle body, during an especially vivid dream or state of absorption.
  - Out-of-body experience (during which you may see your own body) after which you report events that could not be known to you in ordinary circumstances.
- Cognition
  - Correctly sensing unexpected danger.
  - Correctly anticipating a melody before it comes on the radio, or a dramatic event before it happens, or a sentence before a companion says it.
  - Apprehending an exceptionally complex and original set of ideas all at once, in conjunction with great excitement and joy.

- Volition
  - Waking from sleep at a designated moment without assistance from an alarm.
  - Ability to control your dreams. (I added this example.)
- Individuation and Sense of Self
  - Experiencing an identity that self-evidently existed before your birth and that will outlast your body's death.
- Love
  - Seeing new beauty and possibilities for growth in someone of long acquaintance.
- Bodily Structures, States, and Processes
  - Sensing an opening in the body—located perhaps between the eyes around the heart, near the navel, or at the base of the spine—through which energy is flowing.
  - Spontaneous rushes of energy up and down the spine, spiraling around the torso, or rising from the soles of the feet.
  - Sensing an extraordinary lightness while moving or at rest, or a sense of elevation from the ground.

Many people have experienced one or more phenomenon in each category at various times of their lives. In fact, it's a rare person who has not experienced one or more of the phenomenon on Murphy's list and then communicated this experience to a friend or loved one. These experiences occur so frequently that sharing them is not uncommon.

When people exchange confidences about metanormal experiences held in common, they are usually so excited by the fact of learning they share a common experience of this type with another human being, they don't stop to wonder about the many different experiences of this nature that they don't share. What does this mean? It means that instead of limiting ourselves to feeling excited over shared experiences, we should take the next step: We should begin to explore *why* we don't share exactly the same experiences right down the line with every human being, why we can't control these experiences, and why these experiences are so varied and, in many cases, so uncontrollable.

The subset of experiences I described is probably not shared one-for-one by anyone else. I'm sure that every reader of Murphy's book could compile his own list, and it would be different than mine. Each individual list would be only a subset of the many possibilities cited in his book. Each person would have his own set. And that's fine. But would haphazard, consistently inconsistent results be acceptable in the domain of, say chemistry or accounting, or even bodybuilding? Why should the *metanormal* be any different than the *normal*; the *physical* any different than the *metaphysical*? This is especially true when we are dealing with the Secret of Life. Wouldn't we want the results to be the same over and over, time after time? Wouldn't we expect this from the Secret of Life—that it would produce the same results over a given number of subjects? Take Ponce de Leon. Imagine that his fountain of youth made some individuals younger, some older, some men turn into women, some grow hair all over their bodies, and some get sick. This would be pretty disappointing; in fact, it would probably disqualify his fountain of youth from any claim to being the Secret of Life.

So, how do we define the Secret of Life? What does it consist of? What will it do for the individual?

Here's what restorative Golden Flower Meditation did for me:

- Triggered autonomic self-healing mechanisms capable of correcting defects related to neural degeneration;
- Allowed me to overcome all addictions;
- Reversed my self-destructive behavior, allowed me greater emotional control;
- Rejuvenated my body as it aged, keeping it at least 10 years younger than its actual chronological age;
- Heightened and enhanced my consciousness by triggering various metanormal effects and powers;
- Refined my being to the point where I was able to effect a release from Karmic bondage;
- Showed me that the ego persists after death, and provided me with the tools to face death and transition into the next state of being.

How do the results of my experience relate to Michael Murphy's list? First of all, with the exception of the Somatic Awareness and Self-Regulation category, most of my experiences do not appear on his list, at least not in the way of: *Did you ever...* type of experiences. Murphy's list doesn't include phenomenon like physical rejuvenation, the actual taking over of the entire being by a powerful, innate, natural force. These are the kinds of extraordinary metanormal experiences that happened to me, experiences Murphy writes about in the later sections of his book. Secondly, the Life Force doesn't play parlor games; it remakes the body and, ultimately, the entire being. It restores, it rejuvenates; it reengineers; it revitalizes. This is not a minor undertaking, not something like two people blurting out the same phrase in unison.

When I started this work, I liked sharing experiences, talking to friends about the different so-called *spiritual* marvels we appeared to share, but I soon realized that it got me nowhere. It was like idle gossip. Nothing ever came of it, because these experiences were so arbitrary. Even if there was a certain factor of synchronicity, we could never figure out how we achieved these results or how to advance to the next level. That's one of the problems with his list. Are there any items on his list that remake, restore, or rejuvenate the human body? Is there any final correlation of experiences, of how to produce these results—commonplace or extraordinary— over and over, time after time, or of a method capable of producing them?

That human beings can and have experienced the whole gamut of metanormal effects as described by Michael Murphy is certain. That they have found a way to standardize the means of bringing about the most productive and beneficial of these experiences in a voluntary, permanent, safe, and repeatable fashion is not evident at this time. Yet, doesn't serious work in this domain point to this? Wouldn't this be the next phase? If experiences cannot be standardized, the results will continue to be considered by a large majority of people as so much hearsay, spiritual mumbo-jumbo, and idle talk. Now is the time to break new ground. Now is the time to move towards a standardization of metanormal experience and a reliable means of assuring the same outcome time after time over a given number of subjects. My experiences, and those on Murphy's list, are worth nothing if they cannot be induced at will or reliably repeated.

> And indeed, that is what many scientists and philosophers argue: the fact that telepathic empathy (or other extraordinary power) cannot be demonstrated in controlled experiments with the reliability of known physical processes, or that spiritual healing seems to occur independently of observable agencies proves *ipso facto* that such things are figments of the imagination. Even mystical experience is denied its claim to knowledge, given its "subjectivity."[19]

Since it's based on the backward-flowing method, a technique perfected by the ancients over a long period of time, several centuries, in fact, restorative Golden Flower Meditation (GFM) takes the guesswork out of the results—it *objectifies* them; it standardizes them. That is the whole purpose of *The Secret of the Golden Flower*. It's a record of many experiences; many practitioners have used the method and achieved standardized results. That's what an oral tradition is! If a technique doesn't produce results, it doesn't get passed along.

Does the fact that the results are standardized, repeatable, and reliable mean the method is easy to master? Hardly. GFM demands commitment, self-discipline, and concentration of the kind you'd expect from a doctorate level program. To undertake it, you have to master the following important techniques, which, although they are not strenuous in the least, do require painstaking discipline.

The following two techniques constitute the first part of the GFM method and they require physical intervention on the part of the practitioner. In a moment, I will add a third technique (the backward-flowing method), but practitioners must understand that before attempting it, they must master systematic diaphragmatic deep breathing and the ability to control the heart rate—two prerequisite Golden Flower Meditation techniques.

Diaphragmatic Breathing & Heart Rate

Although you may not notice it at first, these techniques, along with the ones that follow, are, in fact, similar to exercises we call aerobics. But instead of the aerobic skills learned in the gym amid a cacophony of blaring music and loud shouting that produces a muscular body, these techniques produce a complete transformation of the metabolic and somatic structure of the individual, and they do so in an entirely different environment. These techniques are perfected in a climate of stillness. In fact, the whole object of meditation is to slow the metabolism down so that one's breathing becomes inaudible.

> One should not be able to hear with the ear the outgoing and the intaking of breath. What one hears is that it has no tone. As soon as it has tone, the breathing is rough and superficial, and does not penetrate into the open. The heart must be made quite light and insignificant. The more it is released, the less it becomes; the less it is, the quieter. All at once it becomes so quiet that it stops. Then the true breathing is manifested and the form of the heart comes to consciousness. If the heart is light, the breathing is light for every movement of the heart affects breath-energy. If breathing is light, the heart is light, for every movement of breath-energy affects the heart. In order to steady the heart, one begins by taking care of the breath energy. The heart cannot be influenced directly. Therefore, the breath energy is used as a handle, and this is what is called maintenance of the concentrated breath-energy.[20]

In **Step One**, we encounter the notion of diaphragmatic breathing or the training of the diaphragm to regulate the breath. Since we cannot control or even isolate the muscles of the diaphragm directly, we must find a "handle" that allows us to do so indirectly. That handle is the belly or abdominal muscles.

When we extend the belly, pushing it outward on inhalation and then pulling the belly in to expel air, we are embarking on a regimen of abdominal and diaphragmatic calisthenics. Starting this activity for the first time—whether sitting, walking, or lying down—one may feel a burning sensation. That is the muscles of the abdomen telling us we are beginning to breathe correctly. Using the belly muscles is like pump priming, that is, using the handle of a pump (the belly) to activate the pump mechanism (the diaphragm).

Step Two uses the acquired diaphragmatic breathing skill as a means of slowing down the heart rate, which has the effect of relaxing the body. Again, since we cannot influence or control the heart rate directly, we must use a "handle" to accomplish it—in this instance, we use the acquired diaphragmatic deep breathing capability to make our breathing more profound and more regular. What do I mean by more profound and regular? Profound means still, as in silent; regular means rhythmic.

When we've acquired the diaphragmatic breathing skill, we will be able to take in more air during each breath cycle. How does this work? Shallow breathing merely fills the chest. Deep breathing fills the lungs, the diaphragm, the belly, even the pockets behind the kidneys. With diaphragmatic breathing, we not only take in more air, we slow down the inhalation–exhalation cycle to the point where breathing becomes entirely silent. *The Secret of the Golden Flower* says, "Only the heart must be conscious of the flowing in and out of the breath; it must not be heard with the ears." Like the diaphragm, the heart is a muscle we cannot isolate or control directly. Once again we use a "handle" to control the heart (the source of emotion). As *The Secret of the Golden Flower* says, "The heart cannot be influenced directly. Therefore, the breath-energy is used as a handle."

But why bother with meditation when we have aerobics, bodybuilding, and a host of other exercise programs being offered at reasonable prices in strip malls across the country? Because restorative Golden Flower Meditation is the only method that doesn't wear the body out. That's right, whether you know it or not, although exercise programs build the body up initially, over time they actually wear it out at a much faster rate. Meditation, on the other hand, has the opposite effect; it actually rejuvenates and revitalizes the body.

That's why I call Chapter 4—*Hydraulics & Pneumatics*—to illustrate how Golden Flower Meditation uses the nervous and respiratory systems to trigger a host of metabolic and somatic activity in the human body. Through restorative Golden Flower Meditation, the nervous system is stimulated such that the natural chemical substances of the body are recombined and used for healing and rejuvenative purposes. We'll get back to this notion of wearing the body out versus rejuvenating it, but first we need to learn about the backward-flowing method and how, along with diaphragmatic deep breathing and control of heart rate, it fits into restorative Golden Flower Meditation (GFM).

Are You Ready for GFM?

Before beginning GFM, you must be ready for it. Your state of readiness is not something I, or any other person, can determine. Only *you* know if you're ready; only *your body* can tell you. And it will, if you learn how to listen to it. Here's how GFM works step-by-step, and I include some recommendations for determining your state of readiness.

Check Your Symmetry

Q: What's so important about symmetry?

A: "Symmetry means being the same, or even, on each side. Over the last few years, biologists have looked at the animal kingdom, and they've made a few discoveries about symmetry, and how it relates to beauty and fitness.

"First, animals that are more symmetrical are more likely to attract a mate. One scientist found that he could turn attractive male swallows into unattractive male swallows (and also ruin their chances of a good sex life) by clipping their tail feathers with scissors.

"Secondly, symmetry influences fitness. Horses that are more symmetrical run faster than horses that are less symmetrical. In one study, biologists measured some ten features on 73 thoroughbreds—features such as the thickness of the knee, or the width of the nostrils. The differences they could measure were quite small, and probably had nothing directly to do with how fast the horse could run. In fact, symmetry is probably a good indicator of general health and strength. Our imperfect world is full of nasty chemicals and germs. Only those individuals that are lucky enough to inherit a sturdy genetic makeup, and are also lucky enough to get good nutrition while they're growing, will end up being more symmetrical."[21]

Get the point? Symmetry more or less guarantees unblocked nerve channels and balanced growth.

Q: I'm not symmetrical; what can I do about it?

A: If you're not symmetrical, something must have happened. After my accident, my symmetrical body became asymmetrical. I gambled, and Kundalini restored my symmetry. Now, I didn't get up one day and announce, "I'm off to find the Secret Teachings." I stumbled onto them accidentally. Destiny put me on a course toward my childhood accident and serendipity (a creative form of destiny) put me on the path to discovering and mastering the backward-flowing method. So, however you get there, whether by destiny, fate, happenstance, Karma, or serendipity, if you're meant to get there you will. It's up to you to understand the commitment and evaluate the effort.

Q: How do I check my symmetry?

A: There are various means of checking symmetry:

- Musical ability, rhythm. The ability to sing notes with proper intonation.
- Mathematical ability, computer programming.
- Sports. Especially balancing sports such as skateboarding, target sports, ice-skating, gymnastics, bicycling, tightrope walking, juggling.
- Kirlian photography.
- Regular photography, a process you can undertake yourself. Here's how:

Take a portrait-sized photo of yourself. Scan the negative into your computer, load it into Photoshop, and crop the image until the face is tightly enclosed in the frame. Drop a line down the exact center of your face, cut the image in two, then separate the two sides. Duplicate each side, and drag the two left and two right sides together. Flip the duplicate horizontally and nudge until it's vertically aligned with its corresponding other half. What you have, in each case, are faces composed of two instances of the left side and two instances of the right side, one half merely flipped to complete the image. Here are sample images taken by a couple of Australian teachers. Study each composite image and compare it with the original.

"After much thought an Art teacher at school and I worked out a way to find out. We photographed some of the children and then through a bit of 'darkroom magic' manipulated them. You'll notice that the photos of each child's face is made up of the original photo."[22]

Right/Right   Left/Left   Original Photo

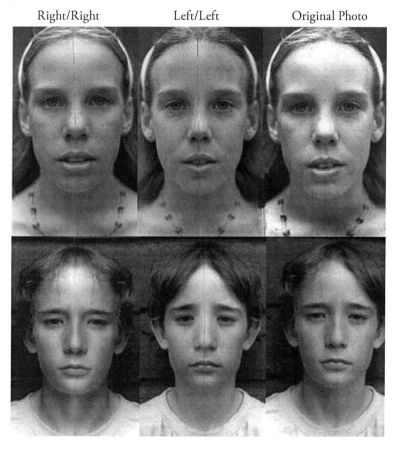

Figure 6: Some faces are more symmetrical than others.

In his empirical wisdom, Gopi Krishna perceived a direct link between symmetry and the qualities leading to success: "Can we deny that whether a fortuitous gift, or the fruit of Karma, in every case there is a close link between the talent or beauty exhibited and the organic structure of the individual."[23]

Note: Failure to pass any of the tests does not constitute a lack of symmetry or mean that you are not apt to undertake Kundalini training. There are other determinants, namely your own resolve and fortitude, but the extent of your symmetry will determine the outcome to some degree. The more symmetrical, in all probability, the more advanced your breathing and lung capacity. Of course, this depends on your physical state, your age, your habits, etc.

Get Clean!

This means including more raw foods in your diet! You can't heal on a poor foundation. This was the one issue hindering both Gopi Krishna and myself. So, learn from our mistakes. By the way, even if you decide not to undertake Life Force activation, this step should be a keeper.

Why? Let's take a closer look at the relationship between a raw foods diet and GFM. What do these two healing instruments have in common? Well, nothing secret or cryptic. In fact, a little common sense reveals that both rely on ingested substances. For a raw foods diet, it's the food and drink you consume; for GFM, it's the air you breathe. One, food and drink converted to a beneficent sugar form; two, elements in the air that your body converts to Prana. I won't go into the science of nutrition or Prana. There are researched volumes of relevant materials. Let's just say that both mechanisms use and refine the elements we introduce into our bodies, so it's up to us to make sure these elements are pure.

GOLDEN FLOWER MEDITATION

Restorative Golden Flower Meditation is culled from my own experience with *The Secret of the Golden Flower*. Is it original? To answer this question, two issues must be addressed.

One, is the method authentic? If you read the chat log in *Chapter 1 - Hidden in Plain Sight*, you witnessed the confusion that *The Secret of the Golden Flower* produces as readers get caught up in trying to decipher the text epistemologically. When I first read the book, I was confused, yet I plowed ahead with the method, ignoring the symbolism and the meaning of the Chinese characters, tackling the method one technique at a time, mastering one and moving on to the next. If my efforts hadn't produced results, I would have dropped it. In effect, I didn't question whether an accomplished practitioner had written the original text or whether the symbols were meaningful; I wanted results. So why persist if nothing happens? Well, something did happen so, ergo, the method is authentic.

Two, given the confusion surrounding the book, should the method merit serious consideration in the modern world? It took me over a year of working with *The Secret of the Golden Flower* to figure out that although the method delivered the goods, it wasn't really viable as formulated. A major overhaul was necessary to make it understandable and attractive to the modern practitioner.

Hence, restorative Golden Flower Meditation, a series of steps containing the techniques that I have already discussed, to which I have added a certain amount of background and explanation:

1. Sit in the Lotus position. Many practitioners ask if they have to sit in the Lotus position. I tell them that if the Lotus position isn't comfortable, try the half-lotus. And if they don't like that, I tell them they can try reclining. The important thing is to be comfortable; there's no point in forcing yourself to be uncomfortable. If sitting in the Lotus position is only going to incite you to give up, then find a comfortable position.

The Lotus position is the optimal position for correct breathing. That's why it's prescribed by so many methods. But the real goal of this method, or any other serious method, is not to learn to sit in a Lotus position, or even the half-lotus, it's to learn to breathe correctly. At the beginning, you want to establish a comfortable posture that allows you to concentrate on breathing.

Drop a plumb-line, that is, find your center as described in *The Secret of the Golden Flower.*

Looking at the tip of the nose serves only as the beginning of concentration, so that the eyes are brought into the right direction for looking, and then are held to the guide-line: after that one can let it be. That is the way a mason hangs up a plumb-line. As soon as he has hung it up, he guides his work by it without continually bothering himself to look at the plumb-line.[24]

Establishing a center is the key to experiencing a sense of your own symmetry. Over the course of your practice, as you begin to master diaphragmatic deep breathing, you will feel your being expand outward from the center point you have established.

I have created a CD called *Diaphragmatic Deep Breathing: A Self-Contained Course in Correct Breathing.* It's available on my Web site: www.lifeforcebooks.com. It will teach you to breathe so you can master the diaphragmatic deep breathing portion of Golden Flower Meditation. You must master this breathing technique before considering the backward-flowing method.

2. Block out the "10,000 things."[25] It is very difficult to control the mind directly; almost impossible to tell the mind to just "shut up" or try what Dr. Herbert Benson[26] calls "passive disregarding." Once again, we need a kind of subterfuge or "handle" to stop the mind from running away. Each teacher has his own approach. I recommend two approaches to "handling" the 10,000 things. Both are attempts to "sidestep" the mind by ignoring it or giving it something banal to do.

The first is counting the breath in a series of four beats: inhale-four, hold-four, exhale-four, hold-four. Start over. Keep counting. It will occupy your mind.

The second approach entails walking, that is, timing the breath cycle over a given number of strides, always breathing through the nose, of course. Inhale-four steps, hold-four steps, exhale-four steps, hold-four steps. Start over. In this case, the activity of walking and counting occupies the mind, especially if you practice in a nature setting, thereby becoming less distracted by the psychic burdens of life and more mindful of nature.

By counting your breath in a regular 4/4 cadence instead of trying to form a *Lotus Petal* in perfect detail or contemplate *Compassion*, you trick the mind and shift your focus away from the 10,000 things. Counting occupies the mind just enough to forestall the 10,000 things. At the same time, it doesn't require you to do something out of reach—like mystical contemplation. As you progress, the counting will fall away of its own accord and your mind will be still.

3. Practice regularly each morning, preferably before eating. As with any endeavor, regularity is a key to success. If you practice every day, you'll begin to notice the little signals your body sends out. Then, not only will you watch for signals, you'll find you are able to interpret them.

4. When you notice air current movement in the lower belly as you breathe (about 100 days in), reverse your breath (*the backward-flowing method*). The purpose of the backward-flowing method is to divert the sexual energy (the seminal fluid or, in the case of a woman, the cervical fluid) to the brain. If you thought it had any other purpose, you were mistaken. This is the Secret of Life—plain and simple.

Although the *backward-flowing method* is the key to making it all work, it's a big step to consider, because there's no turning back. I got confirmation on this fact firsthand, for shortly after I willed my breath to change directions, the Life Force activation process began. Using Golden Flower Meditation to activate the Life Force was a restorative process—physically, mentally, spiritually—for me and for the ancients who studied and practiced this method in the past, as well as for many modern practitioners. Yet, it is a life-changing step. It will affect your being from body to mind, from eating habits to sexual nature. The seminal fluid will be diverted to the brain and used to create a new being with a rejuvenated body and an aptitude for greater metaphysical exploration and understanding. Once the process is underway—the seminal fluid is diverted to the brain—sexual activity and even procreation have a debilitating effort, at least during the first phase. The brain needs a constant supply of this fluid, so you must conserve it.

Diaphragmatic deep breathing is the key to stabilizing the heart rate, but the key to causing the energy to flow upward to the brain is the *backward-flowing method*. It, too, works like pump-priming. Reversing the direction of the breath begins the process of *drawing seminal fluid up the spinal column*.

My familiarity with the backward-flowing method stems from extensive firsthand experience with Taoist meditation, all detailed in my book, *Deciphering the Golden Flower One Secret at a Time*. This book reveals how I was led to the discovery of the Secret Teachings and describes how that discovery was sparked when a stranger gave me a copy of *The Secret of the Golden Flower* in Paris during the early '70s.

I put the book away for over a year. Then one day, as my life began to spin out of control, I started reading the book and meditating. At first, I didn't understand it. Slowly, however, I began to "figure out" what to do.

I became so involved in the meditation that I left Paris to live in a small village in the south of France. The experience was one day, one page at a time; I didn't know what to expect, had no idea there would be such a dramatic outcome. I had never heard of Kundalini, never imagined the human body contained a latent Life Force. This was 1972-73. And Gopi Krishna's books weren't available to me in France.

Page by page, I worked my way through *The Secret of the Golden Flower* until one day, while meditating, I noticed something different in my breathing. In *Deciphering the Golden Flower One Secret at a Time*, I describe the moment thusly:

> Observing my breath as I sit one morning, I am aware that it has the property of direction. At each inhalation the hitherto imperceptible wind in my belly appears to eddy slightly at the bottom of my abdomen as it descends before taking an upward circular course. Or so it appears to me. Down the back, then up the front, in a circular motion.
>
> Something clicks. I remember the words 'backward-flowing method' in *The Secret of the Golden Flower*. Words I passed over a hundred times, never having a clue as to what they meant, never imagining

they might be important. I break off to look for the passage. In two quick flips, I've located the text, 'At this time one works at the energy with the purpose of making it flow backward and rise, flow down to fall like the upward spinning of the sun-wheel…in this way one succeeds in bringing the true energy to its original place. This is the 'backward-flowing method.'[27]

Some respondents ask me what's so special about restorative Golden Flower Meditation. They say any number of serious meditation methods include some sort of sublimation process. And they're right; some do. The difference is that the backward-flowing method works by *drawing* the seminal fluid up the spinal column, not by thinking or visualizing it. What do I mean by *drawing*? I've been asked that question many times. This is a very subtle technique whose implementation begins only at the moment when a practitioner perceives that his breath has the property of direction. This occurs in the lower belly. You may remember that in Step 4 I spoke about regularity and receiving signals from the body. Detecting the property of direction is a perfect example of this type of signal. If you practice regularly, master diaphragmatic deep breathing, learn to slow your breath down until you can't hear it, you will be able to control your metabolic responses— heart rate, etc. Your being will reach a state of total stillness during meditation, a state of permanent attentiveness, a state of inner visualization, the point where breath takes over being. You will be able to observe sensations inside your body. These phenomena are real occurrences. In *The Future of the Body*, Murphy points to them as examples of the metanormalities of everyday life.

When you become aware of this activity—that your breathing has the property of direction—it will put you on notice that the time has come to decide whether you want to continue. Should you decide to go forward, all you have to do is command your breath to change directions. It will obey. Instead of moving down the back and up the front, you will command it to move down the front and up the back—the *backward-flowing method*!

How does "commanding the breath to change directions" work? Recently, a young woman started a dialogue about it over the Internet. She came up with the phrase "directed intention."[28] It's a phrase I think works well to describe the process.

Many people have asked me when they can expect this sensation/activity to occur. Many ask why it hasn't already happened for them. They even say they think it might be happening, but they aren't sure that they are able to recognize it. They ask me to help them.

I tell people that it usually happens about 100 days into the meditation practice, but before it happens, they must master each step, each technique in turn. In other words, there are a certain number of dependencies. How can an individual expect to be able to detect the property of direction in the flow of air in the lower belly if he hasn't slowed down his breath to the point of absolute stillness? If you do not hear your breath, you become that much more able to "feel" it, to become one with it. Once you become one with it, you can direct it.

But you must master deep breathing completely to the point where inhalation and exhalation become totally still. How long will it take to master deep breathing to the point where you observe the aforementioned "property of movement"? Whether it takes 100 days or 365 days, if you want to succeed, you'll have to continue until you can breathe without hearing your breath. Silent on inhalation; silent on exhalation.

As for me telling you if the activity has begun or telling you when it might begin, I can't do that. It's up to you to learn to communicate with your body. What I can say is that if you progress through the breathing exercises and learn to listen to your breathing cycle, you will eventually detect the property of movement, as if the air in your belly is moving. In fact, you will become aware of the slightest occurrences within your body.

The following passage from my book, *Deciphering the Golden Flower One Secret at a Time*, describes what happened when I reversed my breath:

> I visualize a plumb-line and close my eyes. I command the breath to change direction and it obeys. I am elated at receiving confirmation from the book. What I don't yet realize is that this is the last time I

will direct the meditation process. From now on I am on automatic pilot. I remember the words of Ram Dass: At first, *you do it; later, it does you.* Action to attain non-action.

For a week I observe my breath circulate in the opposite direction without noticing any effect. I go back to my uninspired routine: walking, cooking, meditating. Then, two weeks later, about the length of time it takes the backward-flowing process to become permanent, there's something new. On the day in question, I feel a sensation at the base of my spine like the cracking of a small egg and the spilling out of its contents. For the next month, I observe the fluid-like contents of the egg trickle out of its reservoir and slowly begin to climb my spine. What is this fluid? I can't describe it exactly. It seems to emanate from the base of the spine and press upward. Each time I sit to meditate it has risen a half an inch higher.[29]

Why is drawing the seminal fluid up the spinal column superior to thinking or visualizing, or forcing it up the spinal column? Those methods can cause the seminal fluid to go up the wrong channel, a condition that may induce severe pain or cause other problems. In *Kundalini: The Evolutionary Energy in Man*, Gopi Krishna examines this issue in depth.

The backward-flowing method never lets this happen. Why? Because, once again, it's like pump-priming. Changing the direction of the breath kicks off the sublimation process, opening the reservoir of seminal fluid and sending it on its way up the proper channel. It's a seamless, imperceptible, hand-shaking process—the breath slowly drawing the seminal fluid out of its reservoir and up the spinal column.

Recently, a young lady contacted me for clarification.

I always understood the backward-flowing method to represent *urdhavaretas* (vs. merely reversing breath), the reversal of the reproductive center, (i.e., the flow of reproductive essences as a more potent fuel to assist in the awakening thru full Kundalini process of dormant center in brain, known as *bramarendra*). I read *Secret of the Golden Flower*, and connect its backward-flowing method to secrets of *tantric* yoga, as explicated by Gopi Krishna, who underwent *urdhavaretas*. I look forward to reading your book. I am too very attracted to the meditative practice unveiled in the Taoist tradition, as I have problems concentrating, and my mind goes in 10,000 directions.[30]

This is a great question, because it shows how difficult it is to grasp the notion of *drawing* as opposed to *visualizing*, a notion I hoped to get across in my answer:

> As for the backward-flowing method, you are correct, it does involve *the flow of reproductive essences,* or sublimation. So where does reversing the breath come in? First of all, it isn't an issue of "merely reversing breath" versus the "flow of reproductive essences." Breath and "flow of reproductive essences" are sequentially connected. One triggers the other. By reversing the breath, the practitioner guarantees that the seminal fluid will be *drawn* up the correct channel in the spine. Otherwise, how do you get the "flow of reproductive essences" started upward? What is the very first step? What is the mechanism that starts the process? Imagining? Visualization? These techniques are not reliable. They tend to cause problems. If the first step (the trigger mechanism) is *reversing the breath,* then the breath will draw the seminal fluid up the spine, like pump-priming.
>
> The question most people ask after *What is the backward-flowing method?* is *How does it work?* The backward-flowing method is a process with a beginning, a middle, and an end. And like any process, it has to proceed step-by-step in proper order, like a scientific experiment. The first step is to reverse the breath. Reversing the breath triggers step two: drawing the seminal fluid up the correct channel in the spine. It ensures that the process will unfold correctly, without harming or frightening the practitioner.
>
> The whole process is a series of dependencies. Step one "allows" the next step to proceed as intended without adversely affecting the process or the results, which, of course, are 1) Kundalini arousal; and 2) Life Force activation. However, one cannot reverse the breath without first detecting the property of movement in the flow of air in the lower belly (another dependency). And there are others...[31]

5. In a few days, you'll be on autopilot. That is, you won't be able to change the direction of your breath back again. The Kundalini process will continue until the seminal fluid reaches the brain—the third eye, in fact. You will be able to observe this activity. This is the moment. You have entered the *It does you!* phase. The natural Life Force (the Primal Spirit) has reassumed control. I can't tell you exactly what will happen; every case is different, but I can predict that you will begin to observe preliminary effects, such as the magic elixir, the healing breath, and involuntary movements. There are others. The Life Force will explore your body, seeking out areas that need attention. Your auto-diagnosis and self-healing has begun.

Remember to hold to a raw foods diet. This is the most frequent source of problems in this stage, so be sure to stay as raw as possible. If not completely raw, try to include over 75% raw fruits and vegetables in your diet, for they produce the vital, easily digestible energy you need to fuel your activated Life Force. Even small amounts of raw fruits and vegetables provide a lot of energy, including hormones, oxygen, enzymes, vitamins, and minerals. Cooked food provides only the last two elements.

6. Wait for further orders. You have returned the Life Force (the Primal Spirit) to its place of rightful sovereignty. The Self (the Conscious Spirit) is no longer in charge. The Primal Spirit created you; it won't let you get in trouble if you listen to it. Not that the Conscious Spirit won't try to "seduce" you into doing things the "old familiar way." It will. Just sit back and wait for further orders. They will come! Not out of "the burning bush," but from your body. It's the body you must learn to listen to.

In the following chapters, we will study and learn more about cosmology—the role of the Primal and the Conscious Spirits. We will also discover how mastering the Secret of Life provides us with tools for our final encounter—Death. Yes, the GFM techniques you used to activate the Life Force can also be used in preparing for the inevitable. Practiced over a lifetime, these techniques develop a heightened sense of self-awareness, the very discipline needed to navigate what *The Tibetan Book of the Dead* refers to as the *Bardos*.

AFTERMATH

We are accustomed to think that we live in a more or less comfortable world. Certainly there are unpleasant things, such as wars and revolutions, but on the whole it is a comfortable and well-meaning world. It is most difficult to get rid of this idea of a well-meaning world. And then we must understand that we do not see things themselves at all. We see, like in Plato's allegory of the cave, only the reflection of things, so that what we see has lost all reality. We must realize how often we are governed and controlled not by things themselves but by our ideas of things, our views of things, our picture of things.

~ *The Fourth Way* – P. D. Ouspensky

Questions about living with the Life Force are specific to each case. Why? Because so much depends on the method used to activate the Life Force. Applying the wrong method can produce erratic or even harmful results. Moreover, cases of spontaneous Kundalini arousal—those induced without using any method at all—usually leave the individual totally confused. Fortunately, there are many books and Web pages devoted to questions and answers in these types of cases. However, the very fact that so many books dealing with the aftermath of questionable practices exist points directly to the issue of having a safe, reliable, repeatable method in the first place. How does one know if a method is reliable? It is important to be able to describe the experience. Was the experience voluntary or involuntary? Was it permanent, or temporary? Was it painful? And if so, where was the pain located? Was sleep difficult? What about diet? Specifically, what happened? Did it produce the results listed in *Chapter 4 – Hydraulics & Pneumatics*?

Thankfully, by employing a safe, reliable, and repeatable method like GFM, I was able to make a safe landing. Nevertheless, in the direct aftermath of my experience, I had many questions. What were the sensations and phenomena I was observing inside my body? What was causing them? What should I eat? Would I be able to sleep soundly? Would my dreams be different? Would my sexual nature change? Would I be forced into abstinence? Would I be able to come to terms with the force that had occupied my body? Would it hurt me? Could it make mistakes? Would it force me to do something I didn't want to do? Could I make it go away? Could it run out of control? What were its capabilities? How did it work?

I will address these issues, but first, let me assure you that the Life Force as activated by GFM is benign. Moreover, using GFM assures that the results are permanent. The Life Force is with you for the rest of your life; day in, day out, it will be there. And since practicing GFM is entirely voluntary, you will do so in the full knowledge that the results are permanent; you can't make them go away. The Life Force is there to help, to restore. It isn't scary.

It can't make mistakes. It's like driving a more powerful car, one you must respect. Nevertheless, you will learn to accommodate it. It will prolong your life. *It* cannot run out of control, but *you* can.

CHEMICAL EFFECTS AND BEYOND

Magic Elixir

The body is a chemical factory. Adrenalin, endorphins, cortisone, melatonin, testosterone, endocrine are all products of this factory. When the Life Force is activated, many new chemical compounds come into play. The magic elixir is one of them. The following passage describes my first encounter with the magic elixir:

> I recall a sweet taste spilling into the back of my mouth. I can still taste it—a honey-like elixir. I remember looking in *The Secret of the Golden Flower*, trying to find a reference. According to the book, it's the magic elixir of life. I remember being able to see inside my head, seeing the gland between my eyes open like a castanet to catch the elixir. The gland, in turn, sprays it on my brain.

> Once this happens, the battle stops and all, including the two tentacles, cease struggling. And this gland, or *chakra*, the third eye—whatever its rightful name—turns like a gyroscope, meting out instructions and assigning tasks. Probes touch specific locations in my brain, causing muscles throughout my body to react. It controls the elixir, directing it to designated locations. No longer chaotic, it's very precise; a factory at work. All organs, nerves, glands—even the spear-like tentacles—snap to attention, ready to serve. [32]

I remember feeling like I was somehow inside the chemical factory, able to see what goes on in all the various laboratories of my being. Of course, I didn't know the names of the compounds being brewed, but I understood what each was trying to accomplish. It was right after my Life Force activation. I had gone through a few sleepless nights. I had not eaten for a while. This new activity was the Life Force reinvigorating me, replenishing my body with elements from its own chemical store.

The elixir has the power to calm and sooth, also to stimulate. It is sprayed directly on the brain by a gland in the middle of the forehead. I understood this gland to be the Pituitary, the one related to the Third Eye chakra:

> Chakra is a Sanskrit word meaning wheel, or vortex, and it refers to each of the seven energy centers of which our consciousness, our energy system, is composed.
>
> Chakras, or energy centers, function as pumps or valves, regulating the flow of energy through our energy system. The functioning of the chakras reflects decisions we make concerning how we choose to respond to conditions in our life. We open and close these valves when we decide what to think, and what to feel, and through which perceptual filter we choose to experience the world around us.
>
> The chakras are not physical. They are aspects of consciousness in the same way that the auras are aspects of consciousness. The chakras are more dense than the auras, but not as dense as the physical body. They interact with the physical body through two major vehicles, the endocrine system and the nervous system. Each of the seven chakras is associated with one of the seven endocrine glands, and also with a group of nerves called a plexus. Thus, each chakra can be associated with particular parts of the body and particular functions within the body controlled by that plexus or that endocrine gland associated with that chakra.
>
> Endocrine Gland: Pituitary Gland. Also known as: Consciousness Awareness Center, Third Eye, Ajna. This chakra is associated with the forehead and temples, with the carotid plexus.
>
> Location: Center of the forehead
>
> Sense: Extra Sensory Perception, all of the inner senses corresponding to the outer senses, which together are considered spirit-to-spirit communication. These include, for example, clairvoyance (inner sense of vision), clairaudience (inner sense of hearing), clairsentience (inner sense of touch), etc.
>
> Consciousness: This chakra is associated with the deep inner level of Being we call the Spirit, and with what we consider spirituality and the spiritual perspective, the point of view from that deeper part of our being that Western traditions consider the subconscious or unconscious. It is the place where our true motivations are found, and is the level of consciousness that directs our actions and, in fact, our lives.

It is also from this point of view that one sees events in the physical world as the manifestation of co-creation among the Beings involved in those events.

Element: Inner Sound, the sound one hears inside that does not depend upon events outside. Often considered a pathological condition by traditional medicine, it is also seen by Eastern traditions as a necessary prerequisite to further spiritual growth.[33]

Healing Breath

The healing breath is the name I gave to the following phenomenon. I have found no mention of it in any book. This is what I observed:

> As the third eye battles for ascendancy, a hole opens in my abdomen and a force field of energy shoots out, following an arced trajectory outside my body to my head. A castanet-shaped gland in my head opens to receive its stream of energy. I can feel the muscle walls at my solar plexus pull apart and open. I see the energy shimmering forth.[34]

At the time, it seemed to me that my being needed an extra charge of energy to set the Life Force in motion, to restore it to its place of primacy. When I witnessed my solar plexus open and a stream of energy shimmer forth in an arc, I realized that this was a powerful energy drawn from the lower part of my body. An energy capable of being delivered very quickly. It streamed out from the abdomen through the air into the forehead chakra, which then redirected it onto various parts of the brain. This was very precise. It seemed to aim only at specific parts of the brain and avoided others. It had a very powerful effect on my whole body. In fact, as time went on, it appeared to be the cause of certain involuntary movements: writhing and bringing my hand into contact with my sexual organs for stimulation and auto-massage.

Involuntary Movements

These movements are caused by stimulation, usually coming from the magic elixir, the healing wind, or from the energy traveling up the spine. Perhaps other centers are involved. However, I only witnessed the aforementioned energy sources in play.

While I lie there, the energy continues to push outward against the entire inner surface of my skull, and by extension, into my body. After an hour, the pressure increases to such a degree that I start to pitch and roll. My shoulders circle back then forward in rapid involuntary movements while my hands, like artificial limbs, lift then drop onto my belly and rub in swift circular motions.[35]

These involuntary movements usually occur at the culmination of my meditation practice on the average of two to four times a week. One particularly interesting coincidence took place almost thirty years after my initial experience when I came across a Web site describing a Taoist exercise, The Deer Exercise. This exercise is used to forestall the advent of prostate problems, and I include it not only for its relevance and therapeutic value, but also to show once again how the Life Force can trigger an effect whose origin only becomes clear later on, as you work your way through a series of dependencies, in this case, from effect to cause.

The Deer Exercise

The Deer Exercise[36] achieves four important objectives. First, it builds up the tissues of the sexual organs. Second, it draws energy up through six of the Seven Glands of the body into the pineal gland to elevate spirituality. (There is a hormone pathway that leads from the prostate, connects with the adrenal glands, and continues on to the other glands.) Concurrently, blood circulation in the abdominal area is increased. This rush of blood helps transport the nutrients and energy of the semen to the rest of the body.

When energy is brought up into the pineal gland, a chill or tingling sensation is felt to ascend through the spine to reach the head. It feels a little like an orgasm. If you feel a sensation in the area of the pineal gland, but do not feel the tingling sensation in the middle of the back, do not worry. Your sensitivity will increase with experience. If after some time you still cannot sense the progress of energy, certain problems must be taken care of first.

Self-determination is the third benefit derived from the Deer Exercise. If one gland in the Seven Gland system is functioning below par, the energy shooting up the spine will stop there. A weakness is indicated, and special attention should be given to that area. For example, if the thymus gland is functioning poorly, the energy will stop there. The energy will continue to stop there until the thymus gland is healed. When the thymus is again functioning normally, the energy will then move further up along the spine toward the pineal gland. If the energy moves all the way up to your head during the Deer Exercise, it indicates that all the Seven Glands are functioning well and that there is no energy blockage in the body. If you do not feel anything during the Deer Exercise, a blockage is indicated. The movement of energy can be felt by everyone if no dysfunctions are encountered.

The fourth benefit of the Deer Exercise is that it builds up sexual ability and enables the man to prolong sexual intercourse. During "ordinary" intercourse, the prostate swells with semen to maximum size before ejaculating. During ejaculation, the prostate shoots out its contents in a series of contractions. Then, sexual intercourse ends. With nothing left to ejaculate, induce contractions, or maintain an erection (energy is lost during ejaculation), the man cannot continue to make love. But, if he uses the Deer Exercise to pump semen out of the prostate in small doses, pumping it in the other direction into the other glands and blood vessels, he can prolong intercourse.

Under ordinary circumstances, when the Deer Exercise is not used during intercourse, it will be harmful to interrupt an orgasm or prolong intercourse by ordinary means. Under ordinary means, the prostate remains expanded for a long time, unrelieved by the pumping action of the ejaculation, until the semen is carried away by the bloodstream. But the prostate is somewhat like a rubber band: it must be allowed to snap back to its original form; otherwise, continuous extension will bring about a loss of elasticity. When the prostate loses its elasticity, its function is impaired and it is damaged. The Deer Exercise prolongs orgasm and intercourse, but it protects the prostate by relieving it.

The Deer Exercise is a physical exercise as well as a mental and spiritual exercise. It improves one's sexual abilities as it builds up the energy reserves within the body. Over time, the mental processes are heightened as well, and the outcome is often a glowing feeling of inner tranquility, which is a necessary prerequisite for the unfolding of the golden flower.

This exercise may be done standing, sitting, or lying down.

First Stage — The purpose of the first stage is to encourage semen production.

Rub the palms of your hands together vigorously. This creates heat in your hands by bringing the energy of your body into your hands and palms.

With your right hand, cup your testicles so that the palm of your hand completely covers them. (The exercise is best done without clothing.) Do not squeeze, but apply a slight pressure, and be aware of the heat from your hand.

Place the palm of your left hand on the area of the pubis, one inch below the navel.

With a slight pressure so that a gentle warmth begins to build in the area of the pubis, move your left hand in clockwise or counterclockwise circles eighty-one times.

Rub your hands together vigorously again.

Reverse the position of your hands so that your left hand cups the testicles and your right hand is on the pubis. Repeat the circular rubbing in the opposite direction another eighty-one times. Concentrate on what you are doing, and feel the warmth grow. For all Taoist exercises, it is very important — indeed, it is necessary — that you concentrate on the purpose of the physical motions, for doing so will enhance the results. It will unify the body and mind, and bring full power to the purpose. Never try to use the mind to force the natural processes by imagining fires growing in the pubic area, or any other area. This is dangerous.

Second Stage — Tighten the muscles around the anus and draw them up and in. When done properly, it will feel as if air is being drawn up to your rectum, or as if the entire anal area is being drawn in and upward. Tighten as hard as you can and hold as long as you are able to do so comfortably.

Stop and relax a moment.

Repeat the anal contractions. Do this as many times as you can without feeling discomfort.

As you do the second stage of the exercise, concentrate on feeling a tingling sensation (similar to an electric shock) ascend along the pathway of the Seven Glands. The sensation lasts for fractions of a second and results naturally. Do not try to force this with mental images.

Some teachings suggest that thoughts should be used to help or guide energy flow. Those who make these suggestions misunderstand the nature of energy.[37]

There are six forms of energy: mechanical, heat, sound, radiant, atomic, and electrical. We emit electrical energy. The electrical energy in man differs drastically from that used to run a house, for example. The electrical current in the average house fluctuates at 60 cycles per second; in men, 49,000,000 cycles per second. The latter figure is about half that of light, which travels at 186,000 miles per second. So when a man starts to think or breathe, the electrical energy will have already reached its destination. Our thoughts, breaths, etc., are too slow to guide the flow of electrical energy.

What occurs at the unconscious level was not meant to be subject to the control of the conscious mind. If the conscious mind interferes with something which through evolution it was not meant to control — helping or guiding electrical energy through visualization, thoughts, etc. — it can cause a great deal of damage. Its interference with the natural progress of energy can cause schizophrenia, brain damage, and a host of other problems. Taoists call these calamities "Disintegration into Evil."

The Deer Exercise is extremely safe — provided, that is, it is not supplemented with techniques of other teachings. For show, various incompatible techniques are often thrown together to create spectacular techniques, but the results are often disastrous. Lao-Tse said, "My way is simple and easy." And true Taoist methods ARE simple and easy.

NOTE A: At first you may find that you are able to hold the anal sphincter muscles tight for only a few seconds. Please persist. After several weeks you will be able to hold the muscles tight for quite awhile without experiencing weariness or strain.

NOTE B: To determine whether the Deer Exercise is having an effect on the prostrate gland, try this test: As you urinate, try to stop the stream of urine entirely through anal muscle contractions. If you are able to do so, then the exercise is effective.

NOTE C: Pressure is being placed on the prostate gland as it is gently massaged by the tightening action of the anal muscles. (The anus can be thought of as a little motor that pumps the prostate gland.) Thus stimulated, the prostate begins to secrete hormones, such as endorphins, etc., to produce a natural high. When the prostate goes into spasms, a small orgasm is experienced. By alternately squeezing and relaxing the anus during the Deer Exercise, a natural high is produced without having to jog ten miles or endure the side effects of running.

NOTE D: Do this exercise in the morning upon rising and before retiring at night.

The upshot is that these exercises had been part of my repertoire of involuntary movements for many years before I came across them on this Web site. I had been practicing them for a long time without even knowing that they had a name and a purpose. That's how connected the metaphysical world of the Life Force is with all things natural. My body instinctively knew about these exercises and had revealed them to me as part of an autonomic routine. Now I do them even on the days they don't turn up as part of my autonomic repertoire.

BEFORE, DURING, AND AFTER KUNDALINI

My life has been divided into three periods: *Before*, *During*, and *After* Life Force activation. A narrative account of these periods is contained in *Deciphering the Golden Flower One Secret at a Time*. When I look back at the *Before* period—the long period before I discovered restorative Golden Flower Meditation—I see many different 'I's, a condition Ouspensky describes thusly:

> If we begin the study of ourselves we first of all come up against one word which we use more than any other and that is the word 'I'. This is our chief illusion, for the principle mistake we make about ourselves is that we consider ourselves as one; we always speak about ourselves as 'I' and we suppose that we refer to the same thing all the time when in reality we are divided into hundreds and hundreds of different 'I's. We do not know that we do not have one 'I', but many different 'I's connected with our feelings and desires, and have no

controlling 'I'. These 'I's change all the time; one suppresses another, one replaces another, and all this struggle makes up our inner life.[38] In my mind's eye, I watch those 'I's pass in review like phantom soldiers in a parade of ghosts. I can pinpoint the moment I first became aware of the fragmented nature of my persona. It was in the immediate aftermath of my Life Force activation. I seemed to possess greater clarity, not because I had accomplished a startling transformation. What opened my eyes was watching my body change, realizing that a powerful force had inhabited my body and was rebuilding it. It followed that my persona, my very being, would eventually be transformed as well. It was self-evident.

After ten days, I'm eating plentiful amounts of food, followed by rest, then more food. My head is cracking, reshaping. How is this possible? I don't know. But it's cracking. I can feel it. I can hear the pings and pops. Previously, there was a ridge down the length of my skull. But the front portion of the skull is flat now; the ridge is now confined to the back.

The force I've unleashed is rebalancing the two sides of my person. Is this why Michelle Rubin gave me that book [*The Secret of the Golden Flower*]? Did she somehow recognize my lack of symmetry? Did she realize that the shape of the head controls the shape of the body? Well, it does. I can see it when I lay down, see how the force is pushing my head to fill the dimensions of its template overlay. And once the head is perfect, so will the body be.

At the speed things are moving, it seems like it will take only a few days, yet I fear it's a prodigious undertaking and I temper my elation with caution.

I sleep well. I am constantly hungry, but I have to be careful not to overeat, which for me can be measured in one sesame seed too many. I can no longer meditate in the Lotus position; it has to be done on my back, lying like a baby unaware that growth is taking place while it sleeps.

I am a new person. My anxiety is gone, and the traumatic physical routine of fasting and insomnia ends the moment I wake up. I am in good hands and I feel great.

As soon as I lie down, no matter the time of day, energy surges into my head. The best moments, however, are late afternoon, around 5:00 or 6:00 p.m. Yes, the power is always there and it's clearly up to something. I do not struggle; I have surrendered completely. But what is it up to? It has a purpose; that much is certain.[39]

Well, that purpose was rebuilding and reconditioning all constituent parts of my body, and it appeared to function as follows:

- Once the Life Force was activated, it started working on my body, as if inside me there was an invisible sentience, an unseen source of energy whose sole purpose was to diagnose, seek out, and recondition the damaged and substandard parts of my body.

- There was nothing *spiritual* about this force. I didn't hear voices or see visions, yet this force was continuously at work inside me. Was it intelligent? Insofar as it knew how to go about correcting the deformity in my body, yes, very intelligent. And very deft, very methodical. It followed a plan, took all the time it needed to make sure that excessive force was never applied. Did it tell me what to do? What movies to see, what books to read, what to say to people? No, there was nothing *mystical*, no voices, no burning bush, no angels. I like to think of it as *metaphysical*, an unseen extension of the *physical*, residing inside my body, yet encompassing it at the same time. A benign occupier of the 'I' formerly known as the body.

So, who was I before this metamorphosis occurred? When I thought about it, I realized there had been many 'I's. How silly this parade of individuals now appeared to me. And who were they all? The one thing these 'I's seemed to have in common was lack of reliability. I realized I had my work cut out for me. I had to do away with these various personalities, not so much to reinvent myself, but to make myself a more reliable person, more consistent all the way down the line. I realized that over time the Life Force would steer me in the right direction, not by telling me which way to go, but by showing me what was harmful. Take a drink—feel it in the kidneys immediately. Do drugs or prescription medicines—

realize how the Life Force overshadows any natural or artificial substances.

So where do all the 'I's come from? They come from fantasies, from overactive imaginations: tough guy, smart guy, cool guy, business guy, sports guy, lover guy. Liberalman, spiritualman, patriotman, moneyman. Controlling the imagination may be even harder for women. Society leaves them so little leeway when it comes to meeting expectations. So much is expected from a girl, even at a young age. And fantasies can take over a life.

Morning Edition, January 18, 2008 · Twenty-five years later, a boomerang has come back. Those flying blades are used by Australia's aborigines to hunt animals. They're supposed to return to a skilled thrower. And back in 1983, one disappeared from a museum in Australia's northern state of Queensland. Now an American has returned it. The man identified only as Peter included a check. He also sent a note saying he stole the artifact when he was "younger and dumber."[40]

Since I only heard this story on the radio one morning, I don't know for sure why "Peter" returned the artifact, but I surmise that he had undergone a dramatic personal integration. One day while reflecting on his life, he came across Person A—the 'I' who stole the artifact—and he said to himself, "Who was this guy? Was that me? What a jerk." It took a lot of guts to return it, but it illustrates the point: we don't recognize our many former 'I's until we evolve, until we succeed in controlling our imagination. Once we do we recognize them, we want to get rid of them. Yet, depending on what these various 'I's have done, it's not always easy.

Living with the Life Force is like living in two dimensions at once. You live in the old familiar real world and, at the same time, in a new world centered on the Life Force. You'll need to formulate an idea of what the Life Force is up to, to understand its agenda. At first, it appears inscrutable. But it isn't. You must learn to listen. Not for inner voices; you won't hear any. If you are hearing voices, then something is wrong.

In the Book of Elixir it is said: 'The hen can hatch her eggs because her heart is always listening.' That is an important magic spell. The hen can hatch the eggs because of the energy of heat. But the energy of heat can only warm the shells; it cannot penetrate into the interior. Therefore she conducts the energy inward with her heart. This she does with her hearing. In this way she concentrates her whole heart. When the heart penetrates, the energy penetrates, and the chick receives the energy of the heat and begins to live. Therefore a hen, even when at times she leaves her eggs, always has the attitude of listening with bent ear. The Buddha said: 'When you fix your heart on one point, then nothing is impossible for you.'[41]

This passage refers to a heightened sense of observation, and if you've practiced restorative Golden Flower Meditation, you've already developed this faculty. You have been able to shift from active to passive mode. By this I mean, up to the point of triggering the backward-flowing method, you were instrumental in guiding the process of meditation, that is, you actively worked on breathing and controlling your heart rate. Then you reversed the direction of your breath. That action, carried to its conclusion, activated the Life Force, and *it* started to *act* on *you*. You no longer had to take an active role; the Life Force managed on its own. Remember the Ram Dass saying: "At first you *do* it, after it *does* you!" At first, you might have questioned its taking over. You might have panicked. Instead, you learned to let it happen and as a result, its eventual purpose became clear. At first, it merely inhabited the physical portion of your being; later on, it influenced and determined everything you are. It's the new *You*, or should I say, the new *I*.

Living Underground with Kundalini

There's also an underground aspect about living with the Life Force. What do I mean by that? Merely that if you talk about it, people won't be able to relate to your experience; their eyes will glaze over. On the one hand, you're bursting at the seams, eager to let the world know about the marvelous feat you've accomplished. But if you speak about it, you'll be met with indifference, and indifference provokes feelings of isolation—because people won't understand you. Their vocabularies, their frames of reference, aren't equipped to deal with what you're telling them. Coupled with your own feelings of uncertainty about what actually happened, you may begin to feel that you're different from other people.

Think Richard Dreyfuss in *Close Encounters of the Third Kind*. An extreme case of living in two worlds, and finally being sucked totally into the new one. Well, you can't let that happen, not to that extreme. You have to learn to live in both. You are different. You have a powerful source of energy at your disposal that sets you apart. Or is it just another one of those 'I's? No, it's your real 'I'. But merely experiencing a Life Force arousal and actually letting the life-force 'I' take over the direction of your being demands an adjustment. In the meantime, you may feel like an outcast, an extra-temporal observer, looking at yourself and the world in a new way. You may resent the fact that people don't understand your experience. Hence, the underground feeling of alienation.

My advice is don't talk about it. Learn to appreciate it and to live with it, but don't do a lot of talking. The more you talk about it, the more alienated you may feel. Especially when someone asks you for proof. *How could the things you describe possibly happen?* Well, you might remind them that a crab outgrows his shell many times during his life. Why should it be impossible for humans to outgrow their present body? To search for a means of reconditioning it? Or as Gopi Krishna reminds us: use Kundalini as an upgrade mechanism. But what good would it do to argue? From their present state (never having experienced a Kundalini activation), there is no way that that they can project themselves into your shoes. No way they can see things from your perspective.

After a Kundalini awakening, it takes a long time to gather your thoughts, so take the time to understand what's happening. Save it up for a book. Gopi Krishna waited twenty years before writing his first book; I waited almost thirty. There will be people you can talk to. It will be obvious who these people are. You will find each other. You will also learn to live with being different.

WE ARE THE SUM TOTAL OF OUR THOUGHTS AND ACTIONS

Negative actions also affect the Life Force:

- Ingesting the wrong elements
- Expelling the right elements

Plants need water and dogs love bones; the Life Force also has requirements.

> The Primal Spirit loves stillness, and the conscious spirit loves movement. In its movement it remains bound to feelings and desires. Day and night it wastes the primal seed till the energy of the primal spirit is entirely used up. Then the conscious spirit leaves the shell and goes away.[42]

Just as *the Primal Spirit loves stillness*, at the same time it loves everything natural and organic. Why wouldn't it? It's not something cloned in a laboratory. It wasn't developed in a chemistry lab. It has an aversion to unnatural elements. It also reacts adversely when you expel required natural elements from your body.

How critical is this? The Life Force is powerful, yet it depends on you for proper nourishment and treatment. Remember, if you damage it, you hurt yourself. You are one and the same. The good news is the Life Force doesn't just change your body; it changes your entire being. How does it accomplish this? First, living with the Life Force makes your body sensitive to negative stimuli: alcohol, drugs, cigarettes, bad food. Any ingestible substance that might harm your body. One by one your addictions will drop away. You'll know exactly which substances harm your body and you'll take steps to avoid them. You won't have to fight to break bad habits.

What's more, you'll begin to make better life decisions. Gradually, you'll become a problem solver. You'll be able to live in the moment. To tell yourself, in moments of stress, "I am here now." Or as Ouspensky said, "to remember yourself."

COSMOLOGICALLY SPEAKING

To help put living with the Life Force in perspective, the next chapter explains Golden Flower cosmology. Cosmology is a systematic interpretation of the cosmos, from the macro dimension: the sun, the planets, and the stars; to the micro dimension: the embryo, the fetus, the man; life and death.

I have already alluded to the concept of a template overlay that the Life Force uses to match the body up with its perfect blueprint. The chapter on cosmology clarifies this relationship further. It defines the terms Primal and Conscious Spirits, and explains the cycle of human life, according to the ancient Chinese revelations of life and death.

What I understood from my Life Force activation experience is that these revelations are valid. The life cycle of man actually works just as the Chinese author described in *The Secret of the Golden Flower* some 1,200 years ago. Prior to living through a Kundalini-Life Force experience, I would have laughed at the very mention of this cosmology. Most people do. Yet, it is real.

Why is cosmology important and what does it have to do with adjusting to the Life Force? Understanding cosmology, we can appreciate how our various 'I's and personalities are formed. Cosmology shows us an existence without the 'I's and contrasts it with life as we know it. The two subjects—living with the Life Force and cosmology—are intertwined.

Once you get over the immediate thrill of the awakening, you will realize that your condition is permanent. It's with you for the rest of your life. In a strange, but impartial way, it judges you. Be inconsistent, it will tell you. That is, your body will tell you. Be unreliable, it will show you a sign. Be self-destructive, it will provide feedback. In effect, the Life Force is like a silent partner who always has the right slant on your actions. You just have to learn how to listen to it. It will show you reliability; it will show you consistency. Reliability and consistency lead to fewer fantasies. Fewer fantasies lead to fewer 'I's. Fewer 'I's lead to personality integration and a more consistent human being.

COSMOLOGY

The view that all aspects of reality can be reduced to matter and its various particles is, to my mind, as much a metaphysical position as the view that an organizing intelligence created and controls reality.

- *The Universe in a Single Atom* – The Dalai Lama

GOD MAY NOT BE INVOLVED

Does this mean that the Life Force activation process is not a spiritual experience? First, the word *spiritual* is not an easy one to define. One day I noticed I had been overusing this word. I asked myself if I really knew what it meant— could I define it without looking it up in the dictionary? After all, someone who used it as frequently as I did must know what it means. So I sat down and wrote out a bunch of definitions. None of them satisfied me. After an hour, I realized I had no idea what it meant. Why, I wondered, was this word so hard to define? Eventually it came to me. *Spiritual* was like *nice*, one of those overworked words that have lost all clear definition. I wondered if others were as confused as I was.

A few weeks later, I asked a group attending one of my seminars to write the definition of *spiritual* on a piece of paper. Everyone thought it was a fun little exercise, a nice little interlude. But, as they labored over their papers, I watched the smiles turn to frowns. You know what I got on those collected bits of paper? Twenty-one completely unrelated answers. No two definitions were the same, yet all agreed that they used the word frequently and felt they knew what it meant, even if they couldn't define it.

I asked the group members if they could live with the fact that they did not know what the term meant? Of course, this made everyone uncomfortable. Live without *spiritual* in my vocabulary? No way! So I asked them if they could live with another term— one that might cover everything beyond the material world? After a while, someone came up with the term *metaphysical*. Brilliant, I thought, it's a term that simply means *beyond the physical*. And even though it's not a specific description of *what spiritual is*, it was a term everyone could agree on. For this group, it was more a case of *what spiritual isn't*. Not a lot of mumbo-jumbo, not ten or a hundred different definitions. Nothing subjective. Just, *that which lies beyond the physical*.

In its most primitive form, *metaphysical* is Michael Murphy's *metanormalities of everyday life*, all twelve sets of them.

In an advanced form, it's the practice of restorative Golden Flower Meditation with its ensuing activation of the Life Force, and the triggering of the effects, conditions, and transformations that accompany that activation.

In any case, God may not be involved. Why use the qualifier *may*? Well, because I prefer to speak from personal observation— about cosmology or God or any other subject. And even though cosmology appears to be a vast topic, one sure to be loaded with copious mentions of the word *spiritual*, I want to show how cosmology relates to personal observations.

In the physical world, most everything can be explained, everything can be tested, broken down, and classified. And what cannot be explained today, eventually will be...perhaps. Why should the metaphysical world be any different than the physical? All we need is a method that gets us to a state capable of producing the same metaphysical results time after time, a method that triggers the same metaphysical states, effects, conditions, and phenomena.

With the right "meditational" toolset, we could correlate the observations of numerous practitioners, substantiate them, and form a viable cosmological theory. The only thing is *The Secret of the Golden Flower* has already elaborated a viable cosmological theory in some detail. That's right, ancient adepts used this method to bring about the effects, conditions, and transformations induced by the Life Force activation process. Not only did they use the method, they did so in numbers. Over the centuries, hundreds of adepts substantiated their findings in many volumes. From the *Tao Te Ching* to Gopi Krishna, this cosmology was seen and observed firsthand. It was transmitted orally from master to apprentice. Yes, it was written about; more importantly, it was lived.

The casual reader, one who has not practiced restorative Golden Flower Meditation, may not realize it, but as one who has practiced the method, the cosmological details set forth in *The Secret of the Golden Flower* are accurate and true. The only downside is that they lie beyond the physical where not everyone can observe them.

That's more than I can say for the *provability* of the Apostles' Creed, which is really a statement of allegiance. There's no way to double-check the authenticity of the events, ideas, and notions in the Creed. One must take them on faith. Since Jesus' death, not one person has come forth to verify one single statement.

In contrast, after I activated the Life Force, over time I witnessed effects, conditions, and phenomena that worked exactly as described in the book. And I realized that all observable phenomena in the metaphysical realm could be, and already have been, explained by *The Secret of the Golden Flower* and other books. Not only that, since the death of the Buddha, many people have used these meditation tools to trigger experiences similar to mine, providing empirical proof that the tools do work. But what about those who cannot see or observe the metaphysical dimension? That's like saying, what about those who haven't graduated from college? It would be nice if everyone had, but that's not the way it works: there's a certain amount of selectivity in life, and access to the metaphysical appears to be limited to those who really desire access. But that's still not why God is *not* involved.

The reason God may not be involved is that the Life Force process is mechanistic. That's not to say that the process is somehow less *spiritual* or that there's no Master hand involved. I believe there is. Okay, I used the word. What I mean by spiritual in this instance is the *unseen mechanics of nature that lie beyond the material world.* It's mechanistic in the way butterflies reproduce and evolve. It's mechanistic in the way nature works, and if that's not spiritual, I don't know what is. It's like being inside the growth process, observing nature as it creates basic cells, the way those basic cells are transformed into various types of tissue: muscle, ligament, skin, and brain. In short, *The Secret of the Golden Flower* describes a metaphysical process akin to the mechanics of physical evolution. But it provides a breakdown in behind-the-scenes detail.

The book says that the outcome of life and death depend on a kind of struggle between the Primal Spirit (the natural Life Force) and the Conscious Spirit (the perceiving mind). But it's not a right or wrong struggle, an angel or devil struggle. It's not about morality. It's about what is best for you in a practical, pragmatic sense. For at the heart of the struggle the decisions are left up to you, the individual. This notion of deciding on your own future course—on whether to use the meditational toolset—is not specific to Eastern philosophy; there are echoes of it in the West:

> What dies only once is the "carnal mind," as Paul termed the human ego [the conscious spirit]. He wrote in Romans, "For to be carnally minded is death; but to be spiritually minded [the primal spirit] is life and peace." The carnal mind is a mind that is set on "the things of the flesh." It refers to the portion of us that must die in order for us to put on our immortality.[43]

The life of each individual has two possible outcomes:

1) Procreation (continuing the race)
2) Sublimation (evolving the being)

Remember those church debates about predetermination and free will? Well, if you think about it, in this cosmology there's an awful lot of free will involved, more so, in fact, than any Christian doctrine I know. The debates I remember, at least the ones that took place in my church, always centered on belief. You either believed in free will or you didn't. It was that simple. There was no way to prove it. If you were a skeptic, your mind was open to free will. If you were orthodox, you took the word of the church. There was no such thing as free will, for the church had been campaigning against the notion of free will since the 3rd century. In fact, their message was simple: you had to rely on the church to get to heaven; there was no way you could do it yourself.

On the other hand, *The Secret of the Golden Flower* is an active guide to life and death. It implores you to step up to the plate. It provides step-by-step instructions for succeeding with Outcome 2. Not only does it describe the choices, it explains the consequences of each:

- Outcome 1: Live a so-called normal life; or
- Outcome 2: Experience a rebirth.

Nevertheless, due to a lack of information, most people choose Outcome 1. Not so much choose it, but just go along with the program. In effect, Outcome 1 is the default; life is set up that way. Our survival as a species has seen to it; organized religion has made it the basis of morality.

As for Outcome 2, there are no churches, no official organs, no media outlets informing people on how it works. It's a take-what-you-can-get, find out for yourself program. Yet, Outcome 2 is no less important. The only barrier is finding out about it. Since it's hidden by an information blackout, most people never do find out about it, even those who profess a sincere and devout religious faith. The choices are never presented to them, much less explained.

Both outcomes use the seminal fluid for distinctly different purposes. Outcome 1 for procreation; Outcome 2 for regeneration and personal evolution. *The Secret of the Golden Flower* spells it out. It explains how the Primal Spirit and the Conscious Spirit are active to different degrees in both outcomes. To make Outcome 1 work, you don't have to do anything special. Go along with life: go to school, find a job, get married, have children, grow old and die. Outcome 1 places no restraints on the use of seminal fluid, while Outcome 2 diverts the seminal fluid to the brain for the purpose of restoring the Primal Spirit to its former place of primacy. At the beginning, at the moment mother and father create the embryo, the Primal Spirit invests it, *regulating the formative processes of the body*.[44]

The Tibetan Book of the Dead describes in great detail the choices leading up to creation of the embryo. According to *The Tibetan Book of the Dead*, if one survives the after-death trip through the fifth bardo, one is presented with several options for rebirth. Since the *bardos* are important for this discussion, I include a Wikipedia definition of the bardos below:

1. **Shi-nay bardo** is the first bardo of birth and life. This bardo commences from conception until the last breath, when the mindstream withdraws from the body.

2. **Mi-lam bardo** is the second bardo of the dream state. The Milam Bardo is a subset of the first Bardo. Dream Yoga develops practices to integrate the dream state into Buddhist sadhana.

3. **Sam-ten bardo** is the third bardo of meditation. This bardo is generally only experienced by meditators, though individuals may have spontaneous experience of it. Samten Bardo is a subset of the Shinay Bardo.

4. **Chik-khai bardo** is the fourth bardo of the moment of death. According to tradition, this bardo is held to commence when the outer and inner signs presage that the onset of death is nigh, and continues through the dissolution or transmutation of the Mahabhuta until the external and internal breath has been completed.

5. **Chö-nyid bardo** is the fifth bardo of the luminosity of the true nature which commences after the final "inner breath" (Sanskrit: *prana*; Tibetan: *rlung*). It is within this Bardo that visions and auditory phenomena occur. In the Dzogchen teachings, these are known as the spontaneously manifesting Thödgal (Tibetan: *thod-rgyal*) visions. Concomitant to these visions, there is a welling of profound peace and pristine awareness. Sentient beings who have not practiced during their lived experience and/ or who do not recognize the clear light (Tibetan: *od gsal*) at the moment of death are usually deluded throughout the fifth bardo of luminosity.

6. **Sid-pai bardo** is the sixth bardo of becoming or transmigration. This bardo endures until the inner-breath commences in the new transmigrating form determined by the "karmic seeds" within the storehouse consciousness.

The Tibetan Book of the Dead is all about bardos four through six, and the preparations for transiting through each. In transitioning to **Sid-pai bardo** from the previous bardo, the about-to-be-born faces the choice of deciding whether or not to enter into a womb to be born again. Should he decide to enter a womb, instructions on how to select a womb for noble birth and the fulfillment of karmic destiny are provided in great detail:

> Do not enter into any sort of womb which may come by. Since thou now possessest a slender supernormal power of foreknowledge, all the places [of birth] will now be known to thee, one after another. (In a series of visions, the Knower will become aware of the lot or destiny of each womb or place of birth seen.) Choose accordingly.

Even though a womb may appear good, do not be attracted; if it appears bad, have no repulsion towards it. To be free from repulsion and attraction, or from the wish to take or to avoid,—to enter in the mood of complete impartiality,—is the most profound of arts.[45]

What is the point of this? The point is, as *The Tibetan Book of the Dead* stresses: "Know thyself in the *bardo*."[46] This is important, because knowing oneself in the bardo is a state akin to acute worldly self-awareness and self-control, the ability to resist temptation and illusion. The ability to exert supernormal control and be reborn in a form, state, and condition one chooses. It is also about exerting self-awareness at a difficult time, the moment—immediately after death—when most awareness has fled and the residual being—call it the spirit, if you want—is being lured and tricked by all sorts of illusions and lingering fears. It's about existing in a form and in a new dimension with all of one's tendencies and psychological weaknesses. Tendencies and weaknesses cultivated over a lifetime.

For instance, if you were unable to cope or you had difficulty making decisions during your lifetime, these anxieties will remain with you. If you are obsessed with the problems of friends and family, you will bring these obsessions into the bardo. So the advice given is: *Know thyself in the bardo.* What does it mean? It means recognizing oneself in the afterlife state. It means being aware of one's self even in the radically different surroundings of the bardo, as described in *The Tibetan Book of the Dead.* For comparison, a worldly example of the difficulty of exerting this type of self-awareness might be the exercise of raising one's hands to look at them during a dream. Try it. It's not easy. First, you have to realize *you are you* in your dream. I say this because normally in a dream, we just go along for the ride. We don't try to take control, because dreams are usually recorded POV (point of view), *I am a camera,* style. The dreamer is never an actor in the dream, only a POV observer. That's not to say the dreamer is not prey to emotion during a dream, he is. However, once we realize we can have a separate self-conscious existence in a dream (appear on camera, as it were), we can then realize we have hands and feet, and can cause them to be raised in order to look at them. Step by step we undergo a series of self-conscious realizations until we are finally able to raise our hands and look at them. It takes enormous concentration and it usually takes more than one dream.

Now, think for a moment about knowing oneself in the bardo and selecting a womb. On the one hand, we are being lured by illusion and may jump at the first opportunity of security—the wrong womb. That's when we need to realize we have a separate self-conscious existence in the bardo, that we need to, "Cast away all weakness and attraction towards sons and daughters or any relations left behind; they can be of no use."[47] We have to recognize illusion for what it is.

If, as stated in *The Tibetan Book of the Dead*, this is the kind of self-conscious capability needed to navigate through the bardo and participate in the womb selection process, then imagine how well prepared we might be if we had learned to cultivate this type of self-awareness during our lifetime. That is the *role*, so to speak, of the **Sam-ten bardo**, the third bardo of meditation. If we learn how to meditate, we will be able to realize that we retain a measure of sentience above and beyond our conscious state on earth, even after death in the so-called *Between* state, and that this sentience is embodied in our eternal Primal Spirit. But we must choose the meditation method wisely. Logically, it should be a method that activates the Primal Spirit.

So if, during life, we are able to *familiarize* ourselves with the Primal Spirit, that is, if we learn of its existence and activate it, then how much better off will we be in the bardo? For that matter, if we practice Golden Flower Meditation and self-awareness exercises how much better off will we be during life?

> The aggregate of a living human body, according to some Tibetan Yoga systems, is composed of twenty-seven parts. Behind them stands the subconsciousness, the Knower, which unlike the personality is the principle capable of attaining *Nirvana*.[48]

So if we can become aware that, irrespective of labels and symbolic forms, the illusionary forms encountered in the bardo represent the lingering yearnings of the Conscious Spirit (all the negative tendencies cultivated during a lifetime)—then it is a short way to realizing that the Primal Spirit, this *über*-sentient portion of us, includes all of nature.

And if this sentience is ubiquitous, then who says this sentience plays no part in the formation of our blueprints? According to *The Tibetan Book of the Dead*, we are there at our inception; we choose our embodiment in human form; we are aware of every "*lot or destiny of each womb or place of birth seen.*" If this is true, then the *Knower* is just another name for the *Primal Spirit.*

In the formative stage, before birth, the Primal Spirit, which is without worldly knowledge or consciousness, works as nature's agent, helping the embryo to evolve through the fetal stages. This is not trivial work. It echoes and imitates all of life on earth. Designer, builder, sustainer, nurturer, the Primal Spirit is responsible for the formation of all life. And you know what? The Primal Spirit doesn't know its multiplication tables, doesn't care about String Theory, can't build an atomic bomb or a suspension bridge. That's the role of the Conscious Spirit. Yup, at birth, the Primal Spirit's work is done. It's over. As soon as the fanny is slapped, as soon as the first breath is taken, as soon as the cord is cut, the Conscious Spirit takes over. The eyes open, the ears open, and the nose, the fingers, the mouth start a sensual exploration that lasts a lifetime. We become, in effect, that which we learn during our extended educational process. We are its results. And as we learned in the previous chapter, the many influences we encounter, the many perceptions we have during our lifetimes, create all those various, irreconcilable 'I's. In the meantime, who takes care of the body? The Primal Spirit? The agent that did such a great job guiding us through the bardos, such a great job while we were in the womb? Nope, sorry, he's retired.

At the moment of birth, the Primal Spirit goes into retirement. It's still there, but it's dormant. The new manager of the being is the Conscious Spirit. Awakened at birth, this faculty takes over the role of processing everything the individual perceives in the outside world. This Conscious Spirit sees you through the various stages of life. Mind and emotion are the tools of the Conscious Spirit; tools capable of great things in the material world—but also capable of great blundering. For every step forward, we seem to take two steps back. That's the Conscious Spirit—inventive, creative, violent, destructive.

The Conscious Spirit cannot protect you from the stimuli that start bombarding you at the moment of birth: toxic chemicals, illness, addiction, cultural conditioning, and uncontrollable emotions. In other words, how good a job it does depends on how good a job you do reconciling all those 'I's, integrating your various personalities, holding your emotions in check, *knowing yourself in the bardo*. The Conscious Spirit is easily swayed. And why not? There's so much to see and so many new things to explore.

The Primal Spirit is not native to Eastern traditions; it's part of Western teachings, too.

Imagine you are a prince. One day your parents, the King and Queen, send you on a mission. You must find a pearl guarded by a hungry dragon.

You take off your royal robe and leave the kingdom of your parents. You journey to Egypt, putting on dirty clothing and disguising yourself as an Egyptian.

Somehow the Egyptians discover you are a foreigner. They give you food that makes you forget your royal birth and makes you believe you are one of them. You sink into a deep sleep.

Your parents see your plight and send you a letter that tells you to awaken. It reminds you of your quest to recover the pearl. You remember who you are, a child of kings. You quickly subdue the dragon, recover the pearl and depart, leaving the dirty clothes behind.

When you return to your native land, you see your royal robe, which reminds you of the splendor you lived in before. The garment speaks to you, telling you that it belongs to the one who is stronger than all human beings. You put on your royal robe once more and return to your father's palace.[49]

In this parable, the symbolism is easy to understand. The royal robe, the Primal Spirit; the induced sleep, the Conscious Spirit, the loss of true self-awareness. It's the cosmology of the Golden Flower, only the details are different.

So why is there a Primal Spirit, if it retires when you need it most? Well, quite simply the Primal Spirit is there to facilitate your transition from spirit to flesh. It performs this work many times over. Yes, I'm talking about the Vedic notion of reincarnation, and *The Tibetan Book of the Dead*. The body may die, but the spirit does not. Together, spirit and body make up the being. There can be no purely physical being—not without a spirit. And when the body's time is up, the spirit rises out of the body into a kind of holding pattern. Later, while a new body is being designed, the Primal Spirit facilitates the transition of spirit back to flesh, and ultimately to a new being, trying hard to make the resulting body as perfect as possible at birth, for nature knows that the more perfect the body, the more evolved the being, the easier the life experience. Darwin proved it. Evolutionary psychologists classify it according to laws, rules, and principles. The principles of perfect symmetry.

Yet, while the Primal Spirit is doing its best to implement the plan for your perfect body, genetic weaknesses and other stimuli may intervene. The moment of birth is a dangerous transition, one fraught with vulnerabilities. The Primal Spirit withdraws, leaving the Conscious Spirit in charge. At this time, the numinous plans for our perfect bodies may be spoiled by hostile stimuli—disease, addiction, conditioning influences, catastrophe—lurking outside the womb.

Nevertheless, although the Primal Spirit "retires" at birth, it is still there. Waiting and watching to see if you discover its existence. Waiting to see if you discover the true meaning of free will, waiting for you to make up your mind. Yes, it will still be there after death. It will still facilitate your transition back to life. But, during the time the forces in the material world are creating your personality (or should I say your various 'I's), it's right there with you—on call. It doesn't take sides. It won't be rooting for you; in fact, it doesn't care. It's the evolutionary process of nature that simply goes on and on. Sure, it's powerful; sure, it will help you. It will restore your shattered body, if you want. But take sides? No. Does nature take sides when the leopard chases the gazelle? Does God intervene when one group massacres another?

KUNDALINI REAWAKENS THE "PRIMAL SPIRIT"

One of the biggest problems with Outcome 1 is the individual's tendency to misuse the seminal fluid. Many don't see it until it's too late.

> The fool wastes his most precious gift in uncontrolled lust, and does not know how to conserve his seed energy. When it is finished, the body perishes. The holy and the wise have no other way of cultivating their lives except by destroying their lusts and safeguarding the seed. The accumulated seed is transformed into energy, and the energy, when there is enough of it, makes the creatively strong body.[50]

Make no mistake, the Primal Spirit is the only agent capable of overcoming neural damage or deformity—the only means of restoring you to your perfect body, the only way to resist the effects of aging. And that's why nature keeps it available, in the event that you should someday want to summon it. Dormant, yes; unavailable, NO! Don't you think it's there for a purpose? If there were no reason for it, it wouldn't be there. Evolution would have done away with it.

This practical knowledge has been around for a long time. To understand the origins of these teachings, we have to go back to the time of the Golden Flower, around 800AD. And although it may seem complex, it's a neat interlocking system of birth, life, death, rebirth, and so on. The problem is, as previously stated, not much is known about the Primal Spirit. That's why the individual who chooses Outcome 2 is so rare.

So how does Outcome 2 work? Well, somewhere along life's byways, you have to find out about the Primal Spirit, that is, learn what it does and understand that this agent of life-giving form and energy is still available to you. This is the hardest part of Outcome 2—informing yourself, overcoming a major obstacle: the intentional information blackout that's existed for thousands of years. Where can you find this information? Well, *The Secret of the Golden Flower*, of course; the works of Gopi Krishna; the books of Ramakrishna and Vivekananda; my books and those of a few other practitioners—the genuine Secret Teachings. It helps to understand the cosmology. Why? So you can see how the various pieces of the puzzle fit together. So you can prepare for death. Ultimately, so you no longer need to be afraid of death. The same techniques used to prolong life can be used in preparing for the inevitable.

It's not something one learns about at a young age. At a young age, we're too busy exploring life, mastering it or falling behind, failing and succeeding at various trial and error challenges. Too busy trying on various personalities. Too busy destroying our bodies with drink, with steroids, with drugs, with cigarettes. Too busy caring for our addictions. Too busy repeating the Apostles' Creed.

But suppose an individual gets it together and somehow finds out about Outcome 2, that the Primal Spirit's still around, that it's been there all the time—present but unaccounted for. He finds out how to activate it, what it will do for his body, how it will heal his wounds, forestall the effects of aging, potentially lead to the spontaneous acquisition of new faculties: languages, greater intuition, prescience, etc., release him from Karmic bondage, and finally prepare his psyche for eventual death. Let's say he does all of the above, then it should work something like this:

An individual who states that he has activated the Life Force through the practice of Golden Flower Meditation will almost immediately begin to observe the original blueprint of his body enveloping him whenever he meditates. He will see it. What's more, if he claims to have suffered a childhood deformity or structural injury, abruptly the Life Force will begin to correct this malformation. While meditating, it will saturate his nervous system with a powerful energy that stretches his body outward so as to conform to the dimensions of the blueprint. Every time he meditates, his body will expand a little more. Eventually, after a period of time, it will reach the exact proportions of the blueprint overlay. The Life Force energy inside him will not only rejuvenate his whole being—he will feel and appear much younger than his actual age—it will reconstruct his body, thereby eliminating all traces of his former deformity. From this experience, he will be able to hypothesize that if Golden Flower Meditation did this for him, it will do the same for others.

You see, once you activate the Primal Spirit, it surrounds you like a protective shield, always there when you close your eyes, using the nervous system to search for defects, flooding the nerve conduits with vital Life Force energy, repairing malfunctions, and ultimately completing your perfection.

Is this not a metaphysical wonder? The fact that this blueprint suddenly appears and is used to correct physical malformations? Where has it been all these years? How does it suddenly reappear? Is it a delusion? Hardly, especially since genetic research supports the notion of a blueprint—that creation of a blueprint is part of the reproduction process, a result of the chromosome exchange. Yet this is only the beginning for Outcome 2; it leads to a place beyond where genetic science has yet to go.

Science makes no mention of blueprints reappearing. Or that a blueprint can be stored away in some unknown location during an individual's lifetime. Or why the blueprint is not discarded after birth. Or if it's not discarded, where it resides.

So when does it come into existence? At the split-second before the moment of conception? Perhaps even before? Is it the result of some numinous metaphysical process? Or the work of an Intelligent Design process in nature?

Let's say you don't believe *The Secret of the Golden Flower* or see *The Tibetan Book of the Dead* as relevant. You want to prove this to yourself.

There is a way to find out, namely by undertaking the experiment described in Chapter 3. It would entail someone with a minor structural birth defect practicing GFM. If the Life Force corrected this individual's defect, wouldn't it indicate that the blueprint had to have been created prior to conception? And if this were the case, wouldn't it point to an Intelligent Designer, a sentient agent or entity who intervenes an instant before the reproduction process begins? Well, according to *The Tibetan Book of the Dead* we have the potential of becoming Knowers. And if becoming a Knower is a possibility, doesn't that mean there must be something to know?

Once again, I'm not talking about God. God, as I've said, may not be involved. I'm talking about the mechanistic process that sometimes scrambles an individual's genetic code, thereby causing malformations. In any case, even when a person is born with an imperfection, life goes on. Now if God were involved, wouldn't He, as an all-powerful, super-conscious entity, intervene at the moment of conception to correct a malformation? Tweaking chromosomes, nudging cells into place like an omniscient assembly line inspector? Perhaps I'm thinking too much about Jim Carrey in *Bruce Almighty*, fingers flying across a smoking keyboard, God receiving millions of email prayers and answering them in a few nanoseconds. Unfortunately, that type of oversimplification is pretty much the way we've come to think of God. The ubiquitous quality control clerk.

But that's not the way things work. Most of what we observe, most of what science tells us about the way things work, is evolutionary mechanics. Nature plodding along, taking care of business, species slowly refining themselves, just as Darwin postulated. So even if God is not involved, does that make Nature any less *spiritual*?

No, because the very fact that nature creates a blueprint and stores it, indicates that there's a lot going on in the metaphysical realm. Not only do we as individuals have a chance to learn about it, we have a chance to decide for ourselves—true offspring of free will—whether we want to explore the metaphysical realm. And if so much information—enough to constitute a blueprint—can be held in storage over time, couldn't the plans for rebirth be held as well, the knowledge a Knower needs to choose a womb? Couldn't a plan for all of creation exist in the metaphysical dimension? Golden Flower cosmology sure points to this. The Primal Spirit not only takes care of our birth, but should we choose to trigger it, it also takes care of our reincarnation. Just as the cosmology of *The Secret of the Golden Flower* and *The Tibetan Book of the Dead* state.

THE TEACHINGS OF TWO GREAT BOOKS CONVERGE

How do *The Secret of the Golden Flower* and *The Tibetan Book of the Dead* fit into the cosmology? Very simply, the overriding connection is the eternal nature of the Primal Spirit. It's the Primal Spirit that stays constant during the endless cycle of birth and death.

> In the theory of evolution, the tendency of a germ to develop according to a certain specific type, (e.g. of a kidney-bean seed to grow into a plant having all the characters of *Phasolus vulgaris*) is its "Karma." It is the "last inheritor and the last result" of all conditions that have affected a line of ancestry which goes back for many millions of years, to the time when life first appeared on earth...
>
> As Prof. Rhys-Davids aptly says [in *Hibbert Lectures*, p.114], the snowdrop 'is a snowdrop and not an oak, and just that kind of snowdrop, because it is the outcome of the Karma of an endless series of past existences.'[51]

Whether *during life* or *after death*, the two books show how the Primal Spirit remains a source of straight talk. The bardos break the wheel of life into distinct existential entities, providing a roadmap for the journey to enlightenment/*Nirvana*. Within this framework, one voice is constant—the Primal Spirit. In fact, the being often falters during those periods that the Primal Spirit is under the sway of the Conscious Spirit:

- During life (**Shi-nay bardo**) when under the sway of the Conscious Spirit, the being ignores the Primal Spirit. Sure, there's an information blackout, but that hasn't stopped everyone. Many "stay in touch" with the Primal Spirit through Yoga, prayer, meditation. The degree to which one loses touch with the Primal Spirit makes the fourth and fifth bardos all the more difficult to navigate.
- The lingering influence of the Conscious Spirit can confuse the being even after death, so that the individual enters bardos four and five in a weakened state, prey to illusion, fear and temptation. This is the material world beckoning to the departed one, an unnatural attraction that causes the being to prolong its stay in these bardos. The spirit has

trouble accepting that the material world no longer matters, that the state the spirit perceives immediately after death—the weeping and wailing of relatives—is only an illusion. *The Secret of the Golden Flower* is a complete guide to bardo three (**Sam-ten bardo**, a subset of **Shi-nay bardo**, the bardo of birth and life). It's a roadmap for successful transition to the next bardo, **Chik-khai bardo**. The good news is, once one learns Golden Flower Meditation, it's not like *Groundhog Day*—it isn't forgotten in the next bardo—it becomes part of the immortal Primal Spirit's bag of tricks for dealing with the wheel of life. In fact, by acquiring Golden Flower Meditation skills, not only does one acquire a permanent means of controlling the Conscious Spirit, one also acquires the means of staying firmly on the correct life path, free from addiction and self-destructive behavior. Moreover, Golden Flower Meditation not only activates the Life Force and its concomitant effects, it prepares the novice for **Chik-khai bardo**, the moment of death.

How does it do this? In this book, we talk about examining all postulates through the lens of empirical truth and observation, an approach the Dalai Lama described thusly:

> In the current paradigm of science, only knowledge derived through a strictly empirical method underpinned by observation, inference, and experimental verification can be considered valid.[52]

So, from an observational point of view, how do the teachings of *The Secret of the Golden Flower* relate to those of *The Tibetan Book of the Dead*? There are two keys to this association. First is the light, as in "the circulation of the light," the oft-repeated phrase from *The Secret of the Golden Flower*. The light one sees in the **Chö-nyid bardo** is the same light one learns to circulate in Golden Flower Meditation, that is, once you actually learn the method. Why is this light important? It's important because circulating the light not only provides verification of success in the meditation; it also serves as a kind of conditioning reflex for the **Chö-nyid bardo**.

The dying or deceased man is adjured to recognize the Clear Light and thus liberate himself. If he does so, it is because he is himself ripe for the liberated state which is thus presented to him. If he does not (as is commonly the case), it is because the pull of the worldly tendency draws him away.[53]

Unlike the uninitiated—those who don't know about Golden Flower Meditation and its effects—the initiated will not be lured or tricked by false impressions or temptations in the bardo. They will go straight to the Clear Light. Why? Because they will have become used to *circulating* the Clear Light during their lifetime practice of Golden Flower Meditation and used to practicing self-awareness techniques. The light will serve as a beacon for navigating the difficult **Chö-nyid bardo** and the self-awareness techniques will cultivate mindfulness. Remember, "Sentient beings who have not practiced during their lived experience, and/or who do not recognize the clear light at the moment of death, are usually deluded throughout the fifth bardo of luminosity."

The second key is the blueprint, a type of advanced inner visualization, straight from Michael Murphy's metanormalities *Somatic Awareness and Self-Regulation* category. The fact that I observed the blueprint of my perfect body, witnessed the inner-workings of my cranium, watched the effects of the magic elixir of life and the healing breath, and many other somatic phenomena beyond the purview of today's medical science, underlines the similarities with the observations made by individuals during near death experiences, many of which back up the narrative of *The Tibetan Book of the Dead*. What one sees during extended Golden Flower Meditation practice serves as preparation for similar encounters in the bardos, especially the **Sid-pai bardo**, the all-important bardo of transmigration.

It has been said by the authority cited (*Way to Nirvana*, p. 85) that the birth consciousness of a new celestial or infernal being makes for itself and by itself, out of unorganized matter, the body it is to inhabit. Therefore, the birth of such beings will follow immediately after the death of the being which is to be reborn as an infernal or celestial being.[54]

ADDICTION

Chris Hansen: You know, you look familiar to me.

Michael: Oops.

CH: Why don't you have a seat, please... Michael, right?

M: Oops, sorry.

CH: Michael, have a seat. I want to talk to you for a little bit... How you doin' today?

M: Good.

CH: Do you remember who I am?

M: Mmm, uh-huh.

CH: Remember? We talked once before.

M: Mmm.

CH: All right, we have to talk once again.

M: Can I just go?

CH: I have to talk to you first. What are you doin'?

M: I'm sorry.

CH: You went through this once before.

M: Yeah, I know.

CH: In Riverside.

M: Yeah, mmm.

CH: You came to meet a young girl and we talked about how it was wrong. You were just in court on Friday, right?

M: Mmm...

~ DateLine NBC / *To Catch a Predator*,
Chris Hansen, Host

Throughout this book I've touted GFM as a means for controlling addiction. How does GFM accomplish this? Most methods of fighting addiction are based on reprogramming or behavior modification—a process that "trains" the addict to replace his bad habits with good ones. GFM, on the other hand, doesn't use conditioning, reprogramming, or behavior modification. It uses sublimation, which is fundamentally an internal chemical process. Implemented successfully, it changes the cravings that the addict feels. How?

All addicts—dopers, drinkers, smokers, eaters, gamblers, shoppers, lechers—pursue their addiction to trigger the dopamine effect. That's the element they crave; it isn't heroin, or sex, or alcohol, or tobacco, per se; it's dopamine, a chemical element the body produces and releases into the brain at the appropriate moment. In effect, the reward for satisfying a craving takes place in the brain, not the penis, or the stomach, or any other part of the body.

With the sublimation process, however, instead of flooding the brain with dopamine—the addict's reward for pressing the Pleasure Button to satisfy a particular craving—the body's chemical substances are recombined and used for worthier purposes, such as healing, overcoming addiction, and expanding consciousness. Proper sexual sublimation diverts the seminal fluid up the spinal column into the brain. The introduction of this new element into the brain changes the brain chemistry such that the organ itself—and eventually, the entire being—is completely transformed. Once transformed, the practitioner's consciousness, as well as his worldview, changes. Sublimation utilizes no instruments, no surgical procedures, no sworn oaths of chastity or renunciation, no reprogramming, no medication. It's the result of Golden Flower Meditation. How do I know? I used this method over thirty years ago; it changed my entire being. So, is sublimation somehow a cure for all addiction? Not really a cure; it's more like a chemical substitute, one that ends the addict's craving for dopamine. The sublimation process substitutes naturally produced chemical elements for dopamine. Does it work for all addictions?

Until now, we've tended to separate addictions into two categories, one behavioral, the other substance-based. But what if all addictions, those in the substance category that we term diseases like cigarettes, alcohol, or drugs, and those in the behavioral category that we term moral failures like gambling, eating, shopping, or sex, all stem from the same type of brain activity?

According to *New Scientist* writer Helen Phillips, "Several studies of the brain and behavior back the idea that there's very little difference between what goes on in the head of a gambling addict and that of a crack addict. Yet, there's a common perception that overindulgence in certain behaviors is all down to individual choice. If you are overeating, oversexed, gambling away your earnings or spending all you time online, you are more likely to be considered morally abhorrent than the victim of a disease. Calling these problems 'addictions' has triggered debates about whether our society or our biology is to blame."[55]

Substance addictions all have attendant withdrawal consequences, from physical indicators like sweats, nausea, cramps, to psychological problems like hallucinations, depression, and moodiness. Alcohol sufferers experience DTs; drug addicts can expect physical breakdown and "cold turkey" sessions; cigarette smokers are so hooked that even a serious lung condition is not enough to make them quit. Yet, according to researchers, behavioral addicts suffer from the same symptoms as substance abusers.

In fact, the consequences of behavioral addictions are in some ways even harsher. Not only do these addicts suffer from dopamine withdrawal, they suffer forms of social ostracism. For overeating, there is radical surgery, diabetes, and social rejection. For gambling, there's prison, debt collection, financial ruin. For sex addicts, the ones who commit serious crimes, there is sterilization, prison, and even castration. Yes, in case you didn't know it, radical solutions like castration are widely discussed and promoted. Here's an excerpt from *Slate Magazine*:

> With surprisingly little fanfare, four states recently passed laws calling
> for castration—either chemical or surgical—of sex offenders. Last
> month, prompted by two prisoners who actually wanted the treatment,

Texas Gov. George Bush signed a law letting judges offer castration as an option for perpetrators of sex crimes. Florida, California, and Montana have all enacted more stringent laws to order involuntary chemical or surgical castration of these criminals.[56]

Until he's been caught in some serious transgression, the addict keeps coming back for more, especially since, as cited by *New Scientist* writer, Helen Phillips, "both drugs of abuse and pleasurable behaviors trigger the release of the same chemicals and gene regulators in the brain." That's right, once again, it's the dopamine effect. The craving for chemical satisfaction.

I probably wouldn't have included this chapter if it weren't for the proliferation of one particular addiction—sex. Why? Because it's an addiction that dovetails neatly with my empirical research on sublimation, albeit in an offbeat way. How does sublimation relate to sex addiction? In effect, sublimation replaces coercive legal, punitive, and mental health solutions to sex addiction with a voluntary, nonviolent program of self-treatment.

Now I realize my proposal may amuse some people, because the mere mention of giving up anything voluntarily in our narcissistic world brings out the cynics. *What? Give up my gas-guzzler? Stop smoking, even though it's killing me? Stop gambling, even though I lost my house and had my arm broken by goons?*

I take no position on the matter. I merely offer a lost cause simulation for employing sublimation to combat sexual addiction on a mass scale. Naïve? Impractical? Doomed to failure? Yes, of course, but so what. Here goes.

A FORMULA FOR FIGHTING ADDICTION

If there's a media event that frames the breadth of sexual addiction in our world, it has to be *To Catch a Predator*—the Dateline NBC show with Chris Hansen, you know, the show that ends with pleading denials like, "I've never done this before." The show that breaks for commercial with the guy lying face down on the ground with a policeman's knee in his back.

I don't know about you, but the men, the ones that get busted on Dateline NBC, don't seem able to control themselves, even to the point of ruining their lives. And that's the real story. That after being on the air for months, with all the attendant publicity and buzz around Dateline NBC, bunches of men still show up to meet the supposed 13-year-old virgin. In their minds, these individuals are moments away from rapture and enchantment. Willing to risk everything even though it could be a sting, they are the victims of a fantasy that's taken over their capacity to reason.

The plot's the same in every show. So, why the morbid interest on the part of the public? The only variations from episode to episode are the excuses each man invents when Chris Hansen walks into the kitchen. Are you as fascinated as I am by the men's expressions when he walks in? Jaws dropping. Doom all over their faces. Is there any man visiting sex chat rooms who doesn't know about the show? It doesn't seem so. So, why risk it? Like moths to a flame, they can't help themselves. They're addicted!

Now, the first step to overcoming any type of addiction is admitting. Without admitting, the addict simply rationalizes his behavior, or if caught in a sting like Dateline NBC, makes up desperate lies. But to the police waiting outside with transcripts of the chat logs and handcuffs, there is little room to wiggle out. Still, in they come, one after another.

Part of the admitting process is understanding the addiction. By that, I mean the harm it does to the individual, to those around him, to society in general. But understanding addiction is only part of the solution—because rational people don't always act rationally. In fact, the standard cures, mentioned at the beginning of this chapter, entail reprogramming and behavior modification, techniques that rely on getting through to rational centers of the addict's brain. Most addicts, however, don't care about the sociological consequences of their actions, their own families, or their own bodies, for that matter. And that's the problem with behavior modification. Because it involves admitting, understanding, and acceptance, it's prone to high rates of recidivism. Many arrestees are back in the chat room as soon as the police release them. Why? Because most addicts aren't rational or emotionally stable enough to "reprogram" themselves effectively.

Moreover, whether the addiction is drugs, alcohol, cigarettes, gambling, or compulsive shopping, most addicts are able to get away with or *manage* their addiction for a period. Just long enough, it seems, to get in deeper. That's why it's so hard to admit to addiction. It's easy to fool yourself and others—for a while. The dopamine effect pays rich dividends in the beginning. Life's heavy burdens are lifted and everyday problems seem to disappear. But the curtain always comes crashing down—eventually.

Let's take a look at a hypothetical person in a Dateline NBC sting. To see how he came by the dubious distinction of featured guest on Dateline NBC's *To Catch a Predator*, we need to have an idea of the breadth of his addiction.

1) Our man probably lies about his age.

2) He's married.

3) The women around him no longer satisfy him. That doesn't mean, he's a bad husband or he doesn't love his wife; it simply means he's unsatisfied—for whatever reason.

4) He likes anonymous encounters.

5) Each time he indulges himself, whether masturbation, a chat room session, or a trip through some Asian sex parlor, he's tempted to take greater and greater risks to satisfy his urges.

6) He has enough money to spend on his secret sex life without it being detected by his friends or family.

7) And perhaps most important, he doesn't realize he's addicted.

First of all, two of the men I watched on Dateline NBC lied about their age. There are reasons to fib about one's age, especially in today's climate of age discrimination, but trying to attract a minor shouldn't be one of them. Plus, although I don't know it for sure, I suspect these men spend an inordinate amount of time and money on a vain attempt to appear younger.

Two, most of the men in Dateline NBC episodes appear to be married. I'm sure they have all kinds of excuses for ending up in such sorry circumstances, but once they're caught, not only will they suffer, their families will suffer, too.

Three, they need to conquer. To experience the thrill of the chase, over and over. That in itself is an addiction.

Four, anonymity is a must. Our man doesn't want anyone to know about his addiction. It's pretty embarrassing.

Five, even though solicitation of a minor is a felony offense, he'll probably begin all over again as soon as he's released. Sad, when you realize that these guys could work their way through this or any other addiction. We'll get to how in a moment. But first, let's examine the ways sexual addiction enslaves people, especially young women, all over the world. That should be enough to make most men stop, but it isn't. Yes, even the realization that patronizing a brothel in Cambodia or Thailand contributes to slavery doesn't make a man want to stop. Nicholas Kristof frequently writes about the international sex slave trade in *The New York Times.*

> I've covered wars, riots, and natural disasters, but nothing ever shook me up more than my first trip here [Cambodia], a decade ago. I talked to 13-year-old girls who were imprisoned in brothels. They were awaiting the sale of their virginity. They'd been sold into slavery by their parents, or kidnapped by neighbors. The problem isn't prostitution as such, the real problem isn't trafficking; it's slavery. Every year, worldwide, 700,000 people are ensnared by human traffickers across international borders. I found it stunning that scholars estimate that the slave trade today is probably larger than it was in the 18th or 19th Centuries.[57]

It's a big money business. Where does the money come from? Like the dope trade, a lot of it comes from the bank accounts of Americans and Europeans. But unlike drug money, most of the sex trade money comes from men who should know better, which leads into point six: our man has to have the money to support his habit, especially as he gets older.

Now to seven, the last point. So focused is our man on self-gratification, he doesn't realize he's addicted. And that, like an addiction to alcohol, cigarettes, or drugs, is simply a refusal to acknowledge the truth. Denial, the therapists call it. It's the biggest hurdle because, unlike the other three addictions, most likely our man's addiction to sex happened gradually, so gradually he doesn't even think of it as an addiction. Sure, there may be a little voice somewhere in the back of his head that tells him he could be punished for soliciting a minor. *Yeah right,* he tells the voice, *punished, if I get caught. But an addiction? What's more normal than a healthy sexual appetite? Addiction? Bah, humbug. After all, these girls wouldn't frequent chat rooms if they didn't want to meet older men like me.*

At least with booze—once you've lost your job and you're lying in the gutter, it's hard not to face the truth. With a sexual addiction, however, as long as our man continues to get away with it, he'll experience feelings of euphoria—the dopamine rush. In fact, in another *NYT* piece, Kristof writes that men suffering from AIDS seek out virgins because they believe having sex with a virgin can cure their disease. How risky, or should I say twisted, is that?

Is it reasonable to ask a sex addict, one of the variety of men featured on Dateline NBC, to voluntarily renounce his obsessive sexual activity? Somehow I can't picture these men choosing abstinence, can you? If it hasn't worked for teenagers surveyed in a recent Congressional study, why would it work for confirmed sex addicts?

So what do research, medicine, psychology, yes, and even law enforcement, offer sex addicts in the way of remedies? A variety of tools and treatments, from therapy to medication to sterilization to castration. No need to go over these—that's not the point of this chapter—although some of the therapies actually suggest that abstinence be part of the treatment. Abstinence?

First, we need to recognize that abstinence—the *just say NO approach*—doesn't work. Don't believe me? Look at the track record of the abstinence movement. Read the latest Congressional study. The irony is that while abstinence is 100% effective, by definition, it doesn't work, plain and simple, because hardly anyone sticks with it. It's the equivalent of relying on the little voice in the back of the head every time a person tells a lie, or every time an alcoholic ends up in the gutter, or every time a thief holds up a liquor store. Yes, the little voice is there all right, but the liar, the alcoholic, and the thief have long ago pushed the mute button.

Their addiction has drowned out the voice in the back of the head. Abstinence is believing the little voice in the back of the head can persuade a teenager to back off. A hearty, "Down, boy!" at the point of maximum arousal.

Whether you side with the strict not-until-marriage crowd or the sex-education crowd, abstinence is not suited to men who live in permanent denial, men who don't even know they are addicted, men who always go back for more, in spite of the risk of arrest, loss of job, loss of family, and public humiliation.

Now, what about sublimation, the simulated solution I propose? What is sublimation? Is it a viable method for fighting sexual addiction, one that any rational person might consider?

Well, many of the men presented on Dateline NBC seem normal, for the most part. Many appear talented and creative. They're gainfully employed, most of them: doctors, rabbis, teachers. Average folks, for the most part. The only thing holding them back from completely functional lives is their sexual obsession.

To break an addiction, we need a technique that doesn't rely on the little voice in the back of the head, the conscience, as some call it. Yet, reprogramming and behavior modification—the techniques used by most social services—rely on the little voice in the back of the head, and these techniques, in spite of the many hours and dollars spent promoting them, aren't always very effective. So, why not a technique that's purely physical? A technique that begins with breathing and ends with the rearranging of brain chemistry? That's what sublimation is—a backdoor means to achieving the same goals as abstinence. A series of techniques that don't require psychological reprogramming.

But that's impossible. Didn't you just say a sexual addict is powerless? Since he's unable to obey any moral imperative or to approach his addiction rationally, there's nothing he or we can do. Sure, there are psychotherapies, medications, sterilization, castration, and prison. But is there a treatment the addict can self-administer? And, if there is, why would he choose it?

The harder he works to satisfy the urges that rouse him, the longer he continues to evade admitting his problem, the less likely he'll be looking for treatment. But if he gets to the point of admitting and wants to take control of his own destiny, to avoid entering the system and its enforced treatment programs that include: therapy, reprogramming, medication, prison, sterilization, and castration, there is sublimation. A process with no negative side effects, a process whose cost in dollars is zero.

So, you ask, does this sublimation process change the way a person fantasizes? No, it's not possible to take over someone's fantasies and redirect them. That was the theme of Stanley Kubrick's famous film, *Clockwork Orange*, using drugs and punishment to reprogram an offender. It didn't work; this type of reprogramming blows the mind. Rather than reprogramming the mind, sublimation substitutes naturally benign chemical compounds for dopamine.

Right now more lives are devoted to perpetuating the race than expanding consciousness. It's a choice many individuals are led to, and many others never find out about. But suppose that evolution were to dictate a shift. That because of planetary overcrowding, more and more human beings—especially those beyond their useful reproductive years—decided to sublimate their sexual drives. Suppose they could be convinced of the benefits of such a procedure?

At the age of twenty, we do the things twenty-year-olds do: study, procreate, carouse, fight wars, pursue our ambitions. Suppose that sometime between the ages of thirty-five and fifty, we decided that we'd had enough of these pursuits. Suppose we decided to sublimate our sexual activity, to divert the seminal fluid to more creative purposes. There are many historical instances of this type. I'll go into them shortly.

What effect would voluntary sublimation have? On our lives? On our neighbors? On the world population? On the evolution of the species? That is, if it became an accepted practice. Think about the world today—with so many people sexually active after their reproductive years, desiring to prolong their sexual activity through the use of stimulants like Viagra. Imagine that these people decide to sublimate their sexual impulses, realizing, as it were, that better health, prolonged fitness, heightened awareness, and a general deceleration of the aging process—to say nothing of the spontaneous acquirement of extraordinary cognitions and other metanormal faculties—might result.

Think about aberrant sexual behavior on a mass scale being eliminated, not by outside intervention or reprogramming, but by voluntary effort. Imagine how sublimating the sexual drive could remove thousands of potential sexual predators from circulation. Consider the great numbers of people realizing that they bore a responsibility, not only to control runaway reproduction on a planetary scale, but also to control their tendencies towards aberrance, a huge reduction in sex crimes taking place because men were channeling their sex drives to higher purposes.

Yes, I'm talking about a voluntary means of avoiding enforced programs like mass sterilization somewhere down the line. I'm talking about an evolutionary turn in human awareness, one guided not by chance or by survival of the fittest, but by collective self-interest. In the final result, it's self-interest that dictates a person's choices; not always, but in most cases. But are the changes in consciousness I'm talking about enough to motivate a single individual to select sublimation as a way of overcoming sexual addiction? Only time will tell.

One way or another, we must adjust our sexual behavior to survive, before we overrun our resources. In fact, were we to attempt this experiment on a large scale, it would prove we were, indeed, the fittest, most intelligent species on the planet—able to shape our destiny by channeling behavior in our mature years to more productive purposes.

The fact is sublimation preserves the body, increases creativity, and expands consciousness. Sublimation is abstinence with a higher purpose. It's been around for a long time. In fact, it's part of the religious practices of many ancient sects. So why don't more people talk about it? Why isn't it discussed as a treatment for sexual addiction?

HEALING WHILE IT CURES

We've made a case for using the Kundalini-Life Force paradigm (i.e., sexual sublimation) as a means of overcoming sexual addiction. Now let's look at the process itself. Call it sublimation, Kundalini, Tantra, alchemy, serpent power, primordial energy, cosmic power, Qi, Reiki, or primal spirit; it has many names, but it boils down to the practice of *activating* the dormant Kundalini-Life Force present in every human being.

> "A man's spiritual consciousness is not awakened," said Sri Ramakrishna, "unless his kundalini is aroused." There we have it in a nutshell. It isn't the keystone, but it comes very close. The brain and spiritual consciousness are inseparable. Spiritual consciousness cannot evolve unless the brain evolves right along with it, and this cannot occur, according to Ramakrishna, *unless the kundalini is aroused.*[58]

But are the legends true? Is there a basis to the notion that sex and spirituality are somehow intertwined? Is sexual energy behind *spiritual* transformation? And what is meant by "spiritual transformation?" Well, in the first place, GFM is not concerned with the so-called spiritual, it's about undertaking a series of physical actions during the practice of meditation. Each action produces a reaction, which obviates a new action—a series of dependencies—if you will. Sublimation occurs as a result of actions you take during your meditation practice. Before producing "metaphysical" results, you will have to master a series of physical techniques, such as diaphragmatic deep breathing and control of heart rate. You start at the beginning and work through each technique in turn. Moreover, according to the law of dependency, the way forward will only appear once you have mastered the previous technique. This is accomplished by developing a heightened sense of observation.

GFM is about becoming aware of what's going on inside yourself, noting your observations, and validating them through a series of checkpoints that render you ready to employ new techniques as you uncover them. You start with the physical, and soon, if you follow the method as prescribed, the effects become ever more difficult to describe with the vocabulary of material science. In fact, as you trigger an ever-increasing multitude of metaphysical effects, you will need to expand your vocabulary. Eventually, the process just keeps moving forward on its own.

Let me cite an example. If you're familiar with my book *Deciphering the Golden Flower One Secret at a Time*, you know how the Life Force corrected my childhood deformity; how the process of activating the Life Force unleashed a vital, healing energy into my body. This energy scanned my body, taking inventory. How? The Life Force uses the nervous system in its correctional diagnosis and therapy. Once a malformation or disorder is located, the Life Force mechanism routes vital energy throughout the appropriate nerve channels to the specific body area. What kind of malformations and disorders am I talking about? Chronic pain or headache, post-operative conditions, stress, back pain, neuritis, arthritis, neuralgia, fibromyalgia, nervous disorders, polio after-effects, deformity, any condition exacerbated by nerve damage—typically areas of the body, which for one reason or another, have been deprived of the normal flow of vital neural energy.

What about cancer, diabetes, heart disease, etc.? They are not nerve related. In most cases, they are related to bad diet and lack of exercise, smoking and drinking, addictions of one kind or another—conditions brought about by mistreatment or neglect of the digestive system, the bloodstream, the organs. Disabilities not related to the nervous system are beyond the influence of the Life Force.

To better understand the type of neural disorders the Life Force can impact, let's look at a specific case. An athlete who's suffered multiple concussions over a pro sports career, for example. Recently, the news has been filled with stories of retired athletes, many of them young, who show symptoms of premature brain deterioration. Autopsies indicate that the brains of some deceased athletes resemble the brains of Alzheimer patients in their 80s. These are cases of athletes who suffered such traumatic brain damage that there is nothing the health care system can do for them. They become depressed, unable to function, unable to operate machines or carry on daily life. So the question is: Could activating the Life Force counteract this condition? Could it, so to speak, reverse premature brain damage?

Before answering this question, let's examine the issue of stakes. What's at stake in deciding to activate the Life Force? A good way to measure the stakes is to read my book, *Deciphering the Golden Flower One Secret at a Time*. I faced a condition, not exactly similar to, but as consequentially dire as the conditions faced by the athletes I just described. In my case, the stakes were all or nothing. I chose to activate the Life Force, found a reliable means of doing so, and my decision restored my health and changed my life. Likewise, each individual must evaluate their condition and consider the stakes. In my case, there was no alternative, no surgical, no chemical, no therapeutic way of correcting my deformity. No way except to activate the Life Force.

Now, let's do a bit of extrapolation. Suppose an athlete with the described brain condition decided to practice Golden Flower Meditation. What would it entail? Not much more than learning to breath in a certain manner. What could the Life Force do? Once activated, it would immediately flood the nervous system with vital healing energy, the same energy responsible for individual substantiation in the womb. This energy would be conducted first to the brain and, over time, the Life Force would recondition the individual's entire nervous system, starting, as I mentioned, with the brain. That is, if the method was practiced correctly.

Should one attempt it? This is no esoteric practice; this is a system used for thousands of years. The problem is this system got lost somewhere along the way. I found out about it, practiced and modernized it. Two years ago, I decided to make the updated version of this system available to those who face situations where the stakes are high and medical choices are limited or exhausted all together.

So far we've been talking about conditions to which there are no optional treatments. All or nothing treatments; all or nothing conditions. As individuals begin to practice Golden Flower Meditation, more conditions will be found to be treatable. There will be a realignment of goals.

So, what does the method entail, really? Basically, it involves learning to breath with the diaphragm during meditation practice, a voluntary physical action which in turn, produces a series of reactions that culminate in the activation of the dormant Life Force mechanism. No more, no less. It's an entirely physical process—with a metaphysical result. Whether the result (activating the Life Force) is worth the effort (learning the discipline involved with meditation) depends on the stakes. Here and now, in this book, I tell you how it works, why it works, what you have to do to make it work, and what effect it will have on your life once it *does* begin to work.

However, this is not a see-if-you-like-it, money-back guarantee process; it's a no-turning-back commitment—once you've begun. It is similar to the decision you make before choosing to undergo a surgical intervention. The difference being that when you decide to undergo an operation, the whole weight of the medical profession seems to be looking over your shoulder, urging you to agree, telling you everything will be fine. That's really the weight of social conditioning, telling you traditional medicine is bound to be successful. But will it be?

According to a recent study by the State of Pennsylvania, there is no connection between the quality of treatment and the cost. What does this mean? It means that hospitals can charge immense sums and not worry about the actual results of an operation. There is no money-back reimbursement mechanism; hence, "hospitals are rewarded for providing more care, not better care. Hospitals are reimbursed even if the care they provide is a result of a mistake or avoidable hospital infection."

Think this through and you'll see it has a kind of leveling effect, especially when you consider that activating the Life Force costs nothing and is not fatal.

A moment ago, I mentioned that Golden Flower Meditation consisted of a series of actions and reactions. Now, the first action I talk about is correct diaphragmatic breathing. Does this first action then produce a reaction? Yes, it slows down your breathing to the point where your heart rate slows down. In turn, this drastically reduced metabolic rate allows you to focus on the flow of air as you breathe. After about 100 days, you will recognize the property of direction in your breath as it passes through the lower belly. Identifying the property of direction allows you to change the direction of your breath—*the backward-flowing method*—which starts the process of drawing the seminal fluid up the spinal column. It's a step-by-step scientific process. What do I mean by scientific? I mean that, undertaken correctly, like any scientific experiment, it's a process that produces the same results time after time over a given number of subjects.

It is a series of voluntary actions on your part, each one of which produces a reaction at every step along the way...until the Kundalini mechanism is activated—the *you do it* phase. And when the Kundalini reaches the brain, the result is the release of permanent Life Force energy—the *it does you* phase.

All right, suppose you successfully activate the Life Force. What happens next? In the first place, you will experience an arousal of the whole nervous system. This is the inventory process I referred to previously. Once this process is completed, the Life Force will begin the healing stage. This may take days, months; it may take years. It depends on the gravity of your condition. So, it takes a while. Is that time wasted? Hardly, especially when you consider the alternatives: the former athlete who's become a prisoner in his own body or the person with chronic pain who no longer functions.

What do you do while the healing process runs its course? The Life Force doesn't just change your body; it changes your entire being. How does it accomplish this? First, living with the Life Force makes your body sensitive to negative stimuli: alcohol, drugs, cigarettes, bad food, any ingestible substance that might harm your body. One by one your addictions drop away. The sublimation process works on all addictions. It doesn't happen all at once; nothing good ever does, but over time you'll find yourself losing the taste for the cravings that formerly controlled your life. You'll know exactly which substances harm your body and you'll take steps to avoid them.

The sublimation process changed my being and personality. It produced a total creative repurposing of brain chemistry. The very chemical processes that once marked me for addiction were altered. Instead of dopamine—the chemical addicts crave—my brain was fed a new substance, one distilled from seminal fluid. Sounds strange, perhaps, but if you long for a healthier life and greater overall creativity, you'll marvel at its restorative properties.

Okay, what about my sex life, you ask. How will that be affected? Good question, because there is a trade-off. To activate the Life Force, you have to give up something. As I state in *Deciphering the Golden Flower One Secret at a Time*, I traded my potential to *copulate at will* for the capability of channeling sexual energy into my brain, a trade-off that allowed me to revitalize my entire nervous system, and subsequently rebuild my body. So, once again, consider the stakes. If you want to copulate at will, you'll probably have to think long and hard about this undertaking, especially if you are a young wife or husband, boy or girl, in the prime of your life. If you choose to go ahead, you don't have to give up sex completely; you will, however, have to learn to ration yourself. Remember, sublimation, by definition, means diverting the seminal fluid to the brain. You don't want to interrupt this process once it starts. Like the man said: There is no free lunch.

So, unless you have a condition that requires you to consider drastic measures, or you just plain want to activate the Life Force, you may want to go on with your life as usual. Understand, however, that one day in the future your circumstances may change. Sexual freedom, sexual pleasure may no longer matter. You may have a condition that doesn't respond to traditional medicine, or you're addicted and want to take steps to control it.

Is there an optimal age? Usually the age corresponds to the end of the useful reproductive cycle. That is, you no longer have any intention of having children—sometime in the late '40s, early '50s. Suppose you change your mind later on. Can you still have children? Absolutely. Just remember that your semen is rationed—the brain needs it.

IT'S ALL IN YOUR MIND

In his investigations, Gopi Krishna has found that during recent times there have been very few instances of individuals in whom the serpent fire burned ceaselessly from the day of its awakening until the last, bringing about mental transformations known to the ancient sages of India. Gopi Krishna awakened the serpent fire himself in December, 1937, at the age of thirty-four, after seventeen years of almost daily meditation. He would concentrate intently on a spot above his eyebrows for approximately three hours each morning before leaving for his office.

~ *Introduction to The Awakening of Kundalini* – Gene Keiffer

Unlike the lives of permanently awakened Kundalini practitioners, most people's lives cannot be divided into discrete *Before, During,* and *After* periods. What do I mean by this? Simply that once the Kundalini-Life Force is activated, the individual's life is never the same. What's more, once he starts to assimilate the magnitude of his experience, he will realize that he used to be a very different person. This realization constitutes a figure-ground setting from which the individual can measure the meaning, and even the intent, of his life, by first breaking it down into three periods: *before* Kundalini, Kundalini activation (*during* Kundalini), and *after* Kundalini.

I began to realize that my *Before* period was like watching an ant colony through the walls of a glass tank. Every movement I made seemed to be programmed and, as much as I tried to change the patterns, whether by improvisation or a feeling I could defy Karma, it was, in the end, impossible. I was locked into a behavioral pattern dictated by my conditioning.

Today, I feel that I am working towards a persona that will shape my eternal being. My *Before* persona is a figment of the past; I can do nothing to change it. I am into the *After* period, which has its own challenges, namely living between two worlds: the physical and the metaphysical, living in the material world and living *in* and *with* the *Tao*. How does one do this? If you let it, the Kundalini-Life Force will equip you for it. Not all at once, but gradually. All you have to do is listen.

The problem is, then, not so much coping or coming to terms with the *Before* or *After* periods; they are what they are. The problem is that the *During* period, although still vivid in my memory, is yet so different from the *During* experiences of others. It's the *During* period that has been neglected, in spite of Gopi Krishna's entreaties that we explore new safe and secure ways of activating the Life Force.

Sit around a room with other Kundalini veterans and everyone more or less agrees about their respective *Before* and *After* experiences. The *Before*—a feeling of distinct floundering and even alienation. The *After*—a startling change of perspective; an almost *Close Encounters of the Third Kind*-like preoccupation with new energies and abilities. These impressions are frequently shared; commonality is widespread.

It's the *During* periods that differ so greatly. How did each individual get from A (his *Before* period) to C (his *After* period)? There don't seem to be many factors common to the processes that produce Life Force experiences. In fact, the lack of a safe, definable, repeatable method is what hinders Kundalini-Life Force investigation today.

KNOW THYSELF IN THE CAVE

One of Amazon's Top 50 reviewed my first book, *Deciphering the Golden Flower One Secret at a Time*, stating at the time, "Semple's narrative command might invoke the envy of a best-selling novelist. And his facility with the language, his ability to effortlessly (or so it seems, without effort) find just the right word or expression to make his story vivid and engaging for the reader is highly admirable. Furthermore, the prose is polished and very nicely edited. The book is a pleasure to read and it reads fast."

I am very grateful to Dennis Littrell for his appreciation of my writing skills and for his favorable review. Obviously, he's a very intelligent, cultured person.

Flattery aside, I began to realize that although he appreciated the storytelling aspects of the book, he was generally skeptical of the claims I made about Kundalini.

> He begins with himself as a child who is accidentally impaled with a three-inch long and somewhat thick splinter in his foot. For a reason that remains inexplicable to the very end of the book, Semple does not tell his parents or the doctors about the splinter still in his foot. He suffers a lot of pain. He goes on to believe that the splinter destroyed the symmetry of his body and caused him to lose his math and musical ability. It is only with the beginning of his meditative practice and the awakening of kundalini that Semple starts to regain his symmetry and his sense of body wholeness. The reader however may come to believe that Semple's problems had nothing to do with the splinter, rather more to do with his propensity for self-indulgence, particularly as he enters his twenties.[59]

Here he indicates that some readers may not believe the claims I made about the way the splinter affected my growth. Whether Mr. Littrell himself believes this, or he is stating that others might, is not important. What is important to me in this instance is not so much Mr. Littrell's skepticism, or the skepticism of other readers, but the fact that his comments shook me out of my assumptions that just because I committed the details of my experience to paper, somehow readers would have no problem understanding them, much less accepting them.

> As a young adult he is given to sex, jazz, alcohol and drugs. The crucial moment in his life comes when he gives up all his bad habits, rents a house in a small French town and alone reaches a climax with what he sees as the life force (or kundalini: he uses both terms interchangeably). However while kundalini seems to be racking his body and mind, the reader may suspect that it is the 15 days of fasting, ten of which contained sleepless nights that brought about his anguish.[60]

This statement is typical of the way some critics work everything around to an *It's-all-in-your-mind* explanation. Why can't it be the other way around: that the Kundalini experience induced rapid changes in brain chemistry, which manifested themselves outwardly in the need to fast and the temporary loss of sleep?

I understand his skepticism. I appreciate it, in fact. I'm grateful, because his comments brought me down to earth. I now realize that until the members of a control group use GFM to activate Kundalini, allowing them to demonstrate proof of extraordinary powers—predicting catastrophes *à la* Edgar Cayce, walking on water, transferring emotion or feelings like Milarepa, flying, healing the sick, etc.—the claims about the power of Kundalini will remain in doubt. But this type of "energy control" has already been documented. Through the power of modern communications, such as *YouTube*, thousands have witnessed the healing energy of meditation masters, such as the man known as DJ.[61]

This is only the tip of the iceberg. Nevertheless, as we press forward towards the inevitable widespread demonstration of Kundalini power, people will remain divided into two groups:

those who are predisposed to believe accounts like Gopi Krishna's and mine, and those who are not. If a person is predisposed, he will try to figure out what I'm talking about simply because he's interested enough in the subject to suspend his skepticism. This kind of person is able to imagine a Kundalini experience, even though he himself has not experienced one. He's tempted to investigate, because he feels it will fulfill some basic inner need. He will go the extra mile, in fact. As a consequence, he's more likely to activate the Kundalini mechanism because, unlike the skeptic, he's let his imagination spur him on. Quite an amazing aptitude when you consider the fact that Kundalini operates on a wholly unfamiliar and different plane of reality, a metaphysical plane quite remote from, yet tenuously connected to, the physical, material plane. The novice can only imagine what's in store, yet he perseveres, despite the reservations of those around him.

The metaphysical is a plane skeptics have trouble believing in, because there's been no substantive proof it exists—only anecdotal accounts. But there is a basic flaw in the application of the methodology used by skeptics to refute the existence of metaphysical activity. Notice I say *in the application*, not in the method itself.

The scientific method is an established winner, but it does have a weakness. It tends to label a theory invalid as long as there is no proof—despite the fact that proof could be discovered in the future. Not only does it label a theory or an underlying reality as invalid for lack of confirmable proof, it frequently makes sure that the topic is surrounded with just the right amount of ridicule to diminish its value in the eyes of other scientists and, to the degree it is possible, the average person. Witness the discovery that chills actually induce the common cold:

> For years scientists had been telling us that links between chilling and viral infection have "no scientific basis." Now, according to a recent UK study, they've changed their minds. Wow, I figured that one out for myself at the age of six. Does their turn-around mean all scientific research is flawed or incomplete? No, it simply means that we can figure some things out by ourselves.

I'm not against scientists. They apply a method to prove a hypothesis. A good method, a time-tested method, a method involving hypothesis, proof and evidence. Problems only arise with the method when scientists find no evidence to support a given hypothesis. Then they conclude that the hypothesis is invalid. Sometimes this leads to ridicule. A link between colds and chilling? Ridiculous! How could anybody be so dumb? There's no connection between the common cold and chilling—unless we tell you there is. No connection between Kundalini and neural regeneration, either. No such element as Prana in the air we breathe.

The problem is the evidence is not always right out in the open. It may be evidence one cannot measure statistically or see under a microscope. Does that mean it does not exist? According to material scientists, YES.

But the link between the common cold and chilling has always been there, even before material scientists officially recognized it. So, you see, the material scientific view of the world is largely built on supposition and premise, not on reality.[62]

And since skeptics resist Kundalini on principle, why would they try to activate the Kundalini mechanism? And if they haven't activated it, what can they possibly have to say about the validity and/or truth of the experience—whether the effects triggered by Kundalini are based on fact or not-to-be-trusted anecdotal accounts? What can they know about its effects on the human body? About the nature of the metaphysical plane? About the best method for activating the Kundalini mechanism? Sure, they can read the accounts of others: mine, Gopi Krishna's, many more too numerous to list here. But since they seem to think these accounts are flawed and the experiences are psychic flukes, quite possibly the result of over-stimulated imaginations, intemperate living, or so-called risky "psycho-spiritual" practices, they don't consider it on a scientific par with evolution or chemistry, or nuclear fission.

Continues critic Dennis Littrell,

"What I'm doubtful about is that your experience or the experience of Gopi Krishna had anything to do with kundalini meditation. But it is not a point to debate since such experiences are personal and part of what I like to call private truth as opposed to public truth. The truth of evolution or the fission energy of the sun, etc. are examples of public truth. God whispering into Bush's ear is an example of a private truth."[63]

Interesting, because my experience—when I finally came to understand its full effects—lies precisely in the domain of public truth, precisely in the domain of science. I could, and did, sit down with Gopi Krishna to compare various aspects of our experiences. We were able to verify commonalities. That we were able to do this stems from one factor: We had both experienced permanent Kundalini awakenings. In effect, our private truths became instantly public. Could we have shared our findings with other scientists and psychologists? Men like Carl Gustav Jung? Not likely, for these men do not share our Kundalini-Life Force experience. So, is this then a dodge? Hiding behind an experience that only a select few can vouch for? No, because there are many other Kundalini practitioners who have experienced similar effects. What's more, material scientists are free to join those who have had Kundalini experiences. All they have to do is lower their eyelids and start to breathe; GFM is that simple.

> At the root of the problem lies the fact that we, as a culture, have turned our back on healing.

> "Transformation" is a robust project, and we should not underestimate the magnitude of this task. "We're asking a young physician to become a wise old person, and to do it in 4 years of medical school. That's a lot," observed the late molecular biologist and cancer researcher Helene Smith, who believed an infusion of shamanic knowledge into modern medicine would be a good thing. But becoming a wise healer has always been a difficult and lengthy undertaking, even for shamans. In fact, it was by no means certain that the shaman would survive; the process of transformation sometimes ended in death.[64]

Where is the borderline between accepting a postulate as public truth and remitting it to the "private" sector? I suppose it has to do, first of all, with practical applications. If a discovery leads to material products, it's accepted immediately. If it works, it must be good. This doesn't make it any more true than Life Force Science.

Yet, how many books on metaphysics, parapsychology, and spirituality are sold each year? And how many on physics and chemistry? Yes, we're back to *unconscious yearning*. There's a thirst for spiritual knowledge. What? Has the thrill gone out of science? Why are there so many books about phenomena that can't be observed? Sort of a role reversal with the turn of the 20th Century when so much was written about science and mankind had such high hopes. But more books on a subject don't make it more true.

Certainly, the emergence of spiritual exploration is a reaction to the *ad hoc* approach of science.

> Being *ad hoc* in its approach, Modern Western Science does not look into the long-range consequences and effects of its technological applications on the human mind, social life, and ecology, and, as a result, while it solves one problem, it creates several others more pervasive in their harmful effects, as is often seen.[65]

Yet, I tend to side with scientists on this one: that in order to be considered a science, or even an adjunct to science, a seamless method for activating the Life Force and producing the effects listed throughout this book must be found, not only to lend legitimacy to the issue, but to create the "golden crop of towering spiritual and mental prodigies who, and who alone, in the atomic age will be able to discharge in a proper manner, consistent with the safety and security of the race, the supreme offices of the ministers of God and the rulers of men."[66] This would be the supreme practical application.

Dennis Littrell mentions "kundalini meditation" in his review. But what is "kundalini meditation"? Thanks to the explosion in cottage-industry meditation, it's not an easy question to answer. So, let's begin with a statement by Gopi Krishna from *Kundalini: The Evolutionary Energy in Man*, challenging us to find the "safest methods for awakening Kundalini."

To this challenge I would add Gopi Krishna's findings cited at the head of this chapter that, "there have been very few instances of individuals in whom the serpent fire burned ceaselessly from the day of its awakening until the last." What does this have to do with "kundalini meditation"? It establishes one criterion for qualifying a method of "kundalini meditation": namely, that the method's results must be permanent, not temporary.

What's more, we must realize that when we speak about method, we automatically exclude involuntary Kundalini experiences. Why? Because, by definition, if we talk about involuntary, we are talking about a Kundalini experience that can happen anytime, anywhere, in any set of circumstances, and cannot, therefore, be the result of any method. A method must be a systematic process with documented controls and predictable results. It must be a system anyone with the proper training can apply in order to produce the same results over and over, time after time. Moreover, to be considered, it must be a method that is safe, repeatable, and standardized.

So, what is the ideal "kundalini meditation"? I would say it's a system that is:

1) Voluntary. It doesn't happen on its own account. Its techniques are based on the documented experiences of others. The practitioner chooses to apply these techniques in order to achieve predictable results.

2) Permanent. The results last a lifetime; the individual experiences daily Kundalini-Life Force activity that "burns ceaselessly from the day of its awakening until the last."

3) Safe. It does no harm to the individual. In fact, it serves as "an upgrading mechanism," restoring proper health and stability to the body and the entire being.

4) Repeatable. The method can be used over and over, time after time, in a scientifically controlled manner to produce the same set of predictable results.

Does this mean that involuntary or impermanent Kundalini experiences have no value or validity? No, it means that in order to advance this work, we must define what the work is. Can we not learn from involuntary or impermanent Kundalini experiences? Yes, of course we can learn. But just as a material scientist, who accidentally mixes several chemicals together in his lab, must repeat the process under scientifically acceptable conditions for it to be considered valid, the person who experiences an involuntary

Kundalini awakening must be concerned with the repeatability of his process. If it isn't repeatable, what lasting benefit can be attributed to the process? And if the effects do not last, isn't that sort of like taking off in a flying contraption only to have it crash to the ground after 150 yards?

> Just remember one thing: Kundalini was incorporated into our being for a reason; otherwise it wouldn't be there. So why all the horror stories? Well, I've studied the so-called horror stories, and quite simply most of them stem from the haphazard approaches used in awakening Kundalini. And that's exactly why we should be wary of horror stories. Not only are the results varied, they are often incomplete. Moreover, many awakenings have only been temporary. That's not to say that they weren't useful, interesting or genuine. They were. However, to produce a completely permanent awakening, the method for raising Kundalini must be standardized.[67]

And what is more filled with definable guidelines, systematic controls, and predictable results than Golden Flower Meditation, an updated version of the method in *The Secret of the Golden Flower*? It's voluntary, it's permanent, it's safe, it's repeatable. But it's not readily available; it's not advertised in strip mall Yoga salons. In fact, the hardest part of the whole method is discovering its existence. Imagine trying to do it all by yourself. Consider how difficult it is for a predisposed novice to get started. He or she must:

1) Discover the existence of the Secret Teachings.
2) Realize these Teachings are genuine and entail a meditation practice.
3) Learn and use Golden Flower Meditation techniques.
4) Activate the Kundalini mechanism by correctly mastering the backward-flowing method.
5) Which triggers the Life Force.
6) Which induces in the following metanormal effects:
   - Triggers autonomic self-healing mechanisms capable of correcting defects related to neural degeneration;
   - Allows one to overcome all addictions;
   - Reverses any self-destructive behavior;

- Rejuvenates the body as it ages, keeping it at least 10 years younger than its actual chronological age;
- Heightens and enhances consciousness by triggering various metanormal effects and powers;
- Refines one's being to the point where one is able to effect a release from Karmic bondage; and
- Shows that the ego spirit persists after death. Provides the individual with the tools to face death. Facilitates the transition into the next state of being.

The point is there are so many dependencies, a method must be used. And what about the odds of getting all the steps in order? Step 1, a million-to-one on even finding it? Step 4, figuring out how the backward-flowing method works? Ten million-to-one. And so on. Lots of persistence, lots of dependencies, lots of detective work.

And still I'm asked questions like the following:

Have you practiced kundalini meditation? Kundalini properly understood (and this is never directly said by its teachers or gurus) is an elaborate means to meditation. This is never said, although a Sikh guru who has taught kundalini for years admitted this truth when I confronted him with it. It isn't said because the seeker more readily falls into meditation if he or she believes in the magic. It's like the placebo effect. It would be irresponsible of the guru to tell the aspirant that this is just an elaborate meditative device. You must have read, or at least perused, Avalon's old book and probably some others. Clearly the letters and the sounds, etc., in the chakras cannot be universally "true" anymore than Islam and Christianity can be true in any literal, denotative, public sense.[68]

I read this comment and began to think, "Perhaps my previous book was too personal. I must have done a really bad job clarifying my search for the Secret Teachings and the discovery of Golden Flower Meditation. I know I'll cover the same material in a new book, but explain it in an entirely different manner. Maybe I'll be able to get it across." And then I realized that, no, the method is, and always will be, very simple. Go back to *Chapter 4 – Hydraulics & Pneumatics*. The method takes up all of four or five pages, in a mere six steps. It's not the method, or even the way I explain it; it's Plato's Allegory of the Cave all over again.

Originally, I was inspired by Gopi Krishna's statement in *The Awakening of Kundalini*:

> A few more confessions such as Alan Watts', and a probe directed to the avowals of thousands of human beings who have had the unmistakable experiences of the Kundalini force are perhaps necessary to put open-minded and enterprising men and women of science on the trail of what is the greatest mystery of creation still lying unsolved and even unattended before us.[69]

I thought I had a good story to tell, and by telling it in a personal way I might be able to interest people who were unfamiliar with Kundalini. I forgot about Plato, about the predisposed and the skeptics, and the fact that the method can only be proven empirically. That is, by learning and practicing the techniques of Golden Flower Meditation, which are based on the backward-flowing method, one of the most written-about, but least-understood techniques in all of meditation practice. If you don't actually practice the meditation, you will achieve nothing. You won't even understand what I'm talking about. It's like the prisoners in Plato's Cave Allegory, stuck in a limited dimension, able only to see and comprehend what's right in front of their eyes. Nothing beyond their immediate field of vision exists. They can't see it, they can't imagine it, and you can't tell them about it.

Golden Flower Meditation opens up a new, alternative dimension. Gradually, the practitioner begins to become aware of the internal workings of his body, not all at once, but bit-by-bit. It may be breathing first; next, the heart rate, then, the absence of stress and tension. Finally, other phenomena occur—the sensation of floating up to the ceiling, and turning around to see the physical body lying in bed below. And you recognize it's much more than a sensation; it's real. Part of a new sense of limitless being that somehow extends your body beyond its mere physical confines. Once this happens, you're getting close to applying the backward-flowing method. And once you do, you can't turn back. It takes over; it *does* you. For the rest of your life, you will have the Life

Force managing your body, endowing your being with exceptional aptitudes—untapped resources and extraordinary faculties—previously hidden deep within you.

Understanding Kundalini and the resulting Life Force process has to be approached empirically, one step at a time, as you progress into the metaphysical dimension. As with anything—becoming a writer, a pilot, a diver, a dancer—experience is paramount; talk is nothing. You can tell someone how to fly a plane, but would you want him or her piloting a plane you were in? No, you'd want him to have the thousand or so hours of training and experience. Adequate time to figure things out, time to learn how to learn. A lot of detective work is involved in empirical learning and most of it is done with the body.

People don't like being told they don't understand a given concept, that they must "try the method" themselves. Some may accuse me of using Plato's allegory to condemn everyone that doesn't agree with me. But being unwilling to accept or try GFM *is* an apt example of Plato's allegory. *Oh, it couldn't be real because reality is what's flashing before my eyes. And even if you tell me about it, I won't listen. I won't believe, I can't believe.*

But where are you looking? What are you looking at? If you're facing the wall of the cave, you will never know what goes on outside. You will never consider any proof, anecdotal or otherwise, as valid. In fact, you will never know, one way or another, unless you put your body on the line.

HYDRAULICS AND PNEUMATICS OF THE BODY

Timothy Leary once said the body was a chemical factory. Take the story of the East German athletes of the '70s. Without their permission or knowledge, they were systematically doped with steroids in a misguided attempt to win medals for this relatively small, unknown Communist country. Well, the authorities succeeded. They turned their East German athletes into superhuman, medal-winning overachievers; they also ruined their lives and their health. But the point is: Chemicals regulate the systems of the body. And there are chemical compounds within the body that are more powerful than anything man can invent. Imagine that by using your own organic resources, you were able to create a chemical compound more powerful than LSD and steroids combined, and that this mixture was capable of not only rebuilding your body in a benign and restorative fashion, but also opening the doors of perception to a degree beyond the capability of any man-made or natural drug, beyond our humdrum materialistic imaginations.

This is what awaits you. It is well within your reach. You only have to learn and apply the techniques of Golden Flower Meditation to make it happen—techniques the ancients understood and used to the benefit of mankind.

When Dennis Littrell wrote that he persuaded a Sikh guru to "admit the truth when I confronted him with it," he was telling us that he had taken someone's word for something, which in this work, as Ouspensky reminds us, is tantamount to a person's admitting he doesn't know what he is talking about. "You must verify everything that you see, hear, or feel," declared Ouspensky.

There's enough disinformation already without adding more opinion and hearsay.

> The ancient treatises exclusively dealing with the subject of Kundalini Yoga abound in cryptic passages and contain details of fantastic, sometimes even obscene ritual allusions to innumerable deities, extremely difficult and often dangerous mental and physical exercises, incantations and formulas technically known as mantras; bodily postures called asanas, and detailed instructions for the control and regulation of the breath, all couched in a language difficult to understand, with a mass of verbiage which instead of attracting is likely to repel the modern student. Truly speaking, no illustrative material is available in either the modern or ancient expositions to convey lucidly what the objective reality of the methods advocated is and what mental and organic changes one may expect at the end.[70]

I remember reading this subsequent to my own Kundalini activation in 1973, and saying to myself: "Wow, I've just used one of the methods he's probably referring to, discovered it totally by accident. It's Chinese, not Indian…could that make a difference?" Perhaps. But instead of floundering, getting lost in epistemology and terminology, I sat down and worked my way through the method empirically. And guess what? It worked as advertised. Just like the telephone, just like the toaster, just like Novocain, like thousands of products and processes that do exactly what they say they do. Yes, I had a rough week towards the end of the activation process. But it was due to the effects of my accident, not to Golden Flower Meditation. The fact that my childhood accident deformed me, causing my body to implode, in effect, kicked off my search for the Secret Teachings in the first place. If the accident hadn't occurred, I never would have looked for the Secret Teachings. Now, I didn't get up one day and say: "I'm off to find the Secret Teachings; I *know* they'll put me back together again." I floundered, spent years getting in trouble, feeling alienated, botching my relationships. Eventually I got there, but the accident was a catalyst.

My bodily implosion was caused by the cutting off of vital nerve energy to specific areas of my body, resulting in the degeneration of muscle and tissue in the surrounding areas. As my body began to deform, my whole being changed. On account of the accident, I lost my abilities and my talents.

Talent and ability are closely linked to symmetry. Gopi Krishna knew this because Kundalini allowed him to see the connection. "Can we deny the fact that whether a fortuitous gift, divine grace, or the fruit of Karma, in every case there is a close link between the talent or beauty exhibited and the organic structure of the individual, even though we may not be in a position to specify all the details at present."[71]

On account of the accident, my symmetrical body became asymmetrical. I had, to a degree, imploded. In fact, my body had so imploded that the Kundalini energy, when finally aroused, overwhelmed the capacity of my damaged nervous system to absorb it, especially in the withered parts—those parts to which growth energy had ceased flowing as a result of my accident. That's what caused my sleepless nights and caused me to start fasting— an abundant surge of life force energy trying to circulate through my entire body.

However, once the Kundalini energy entered my brain, it started opening up those withered nerve channels. Within a week, my bodily functions such as eating, sleeping, and exercising were back to normal. I felt fine, a little weak perhaps, but not too far removed from a graduate student who has just finished taking exams or writing a thesis. And once activated, the Kundalini energy started restoring my body. It didn't leave me a psychic wreck; it didn't damage me. In fact, as it began to repair my body, I felt invigorated. I had stumbled upon the backward-flowing method, mastered it, and survived. More than survived, I flourished. Sure, at first, I didn't know what the Life Force was up to, but almost immediately I realized it was benign. A powerful, mysterious, yet benign force with a will and plan of its own. It didn't care about my habits or my routine; it went about its business, slowly reshaping my body, changing my persona for the better, restoring my sense of integration.

So, pragmatically speaking, if a method works, it must be good. That's the grand doctrine of pragmatist philosophy. An approach to various problems and situations tested in the empirical tradition.

In the final chapters of *The Biological Basis of Religion and Genius*, Gopi Krishna recognized the relevance of *The Secret of the Golden Flower* to both the sublimation and the meditation processes. He understood its significance in the search for the proper method of activating Kundalini. However, he was obviously disappointed that the "best and the brightest" had entirely missed the boat as to its true significance:

> The statements of the kind that during the process the semen dries up with suction and becomes thin, that the male organ shrinks, or that the sexual appetite is lost, contained in old manuals, cannot fail to convey important bits of information to the modern savants engaged in the investigation. An ancient Chinese work, *The Secret of the Golden Flower*, contains unmistakable hints about this process, which no one with some knowledge of this process can fail to notice, and yet Jung, in his commentary on the book, entirely preoccupied with his own theories about the unconscious, despite the unambiguous nature of the statements in the work, finds in it only material for the corroboration of his own ideas and nothing beyond that. The same thing happened in a seminar held by him on Kundalini for

which a written summary is still available in the Jung Institute. Not one of the savants present, as is evident from the views expressed by them, displayed the least knowledge about the real significance of this hoary cult and the tremendous import of the ancient doctrine they were discussing at the time.[72]

So what is "kundalini meditation"? Is it the ancient treatises, a hodgepodge of conflicting instructions that confounded even Gopi Krishna, a native of India? Perhaps it's one of the popular methods headlined in strip mall Yoga boutiques. Or is it a system like GFM, founded on the principles of the backward-flowing method? Obviously, the answer depends on what you want the method to achieve. Can there be more than one "kundalini meditation"? Wouldn't that be kind of absurd? To have "kundalini meditation" without *permanent* Kundalini? What would be the point? Well, if you're selling something, the sales are the point. If you're seeking truth, you want something permanent.

Once I realized that the bits of lore contained in ancient treatises like *The Secret of the Golden Flower* could be verified through personal practice, I realized I had the basis of a true modern method, for at the heart of this lore is the backward-flowing method—truly the Secret of Life. Authentic Kundalini meditation works safely and permanently, inducing the extraordinary metanormal effects cited throughout this book.

Permanent, Voluntary, Safe, Repeatable are the watchwords of Life Force Science, not, *it's all in your mind.* As more and more people yearn for and explore the metaphysical world, *it's all in your mind* expresses neither the breadth of their unconscious yearning nor the life experiences that brought them to the point of discovery. To them, a word of guidance: proceed methodically, as a scientist would—a Life Force scientist.

Permanent, Voluntary, Safe, Repeatable.

ENDNOTES

1   *The Secret of the Golden Flower* - Routledge & Kegan Paul, Wilhelm Translation, p. 62.
2   "The Big View" http://www.thebigview.com/forum/index.php?s=e7d 9ce8a754edba4138ec0deb418eaa8 - This exchange is a sample of the continuing fascination with the meaning of, and various approaches to, *The Secret of the Golden Flower*. Similar discussions exist in books and throughout the Internet.
3   I include a link to some Amazon comments on the Wilhelm translation hereafter: http://www.amazon.com/Secret-Golden-Flower-Chinese-Book/dp/0156799804/ref=pd_bxgy_b_img_b
4   The Chinese name for *The Secret of the Golden Flower*.
5   Amazon.com comments on the Cleary translation http://www.amazon.com/review/product/0062501933/ref=cm_cr_dp_all_helpful?%5Fencoding=UTF8&coliid=&showViewpoints=1&colid=&sortBy=bySubmissionDateDescending
   By O. Au "oscarau" (UK) I have not modified the original:
   This book is a good new English translation of the original Chinese text, and nothing more. The reader has to be familiar with Taoist text to unlock the full secret of the golden flower. Cleary seems to have a personal grudge against the translator of the original English version of this book and in doing so it leaves the reader disillusioned as to what exactly is the secret.
   If you like Taoist literature, this book is invaluable, but if you want to learn the meditation techniques, get you hands on Wilhelm's original translation. Better explanations can be had from the Wilhelm.
6   *The Fourth Way* – P.D. Ouspensky, Knopf, 1957.
7   "Let Us Get Drunk and Meditate: Here is your Zen green-tea liqueur and your Enlightenment Visa card. Go forth and levitate" - Mark

Morford, SF Gate, *San Francisco Observer*, Wednesday, October 10, 2007.

8 *Cosmic Consciousness* – Richard Bucke, University Books, 1961.

9 *The Future of the Body* – Michael Murphy, Tarcher/Putnam 1992, p. 30.

10 *The Stanford Encyclopedia of Knowledge*, <http://plato.stanford.edu/entries/rationalism-empiricism/>

11 "Redskins' Season Turns Around" - Ben Shpigel, *Washington Post*, Published: December 31, 2007. http://www.nytimes.com/2007/12/31/sports/football/31redskins.html?pagewanted=all

12 *Reincarnation: The Missing Link in Christianity* - Elizabeth Clare Prophet, Summit University Press, 1997, pp. 91-92.

13 Ibid, p. 198.

14 *Deciphering the Golden Flower One Secret at a Time* – JJ Semple, Life Force Books, 2007, p. xiii.

15 "Judgment Day: Intelligent Design on Trial" - NOVA, Original PBS Broadcast Date: November 13, 2007.

16 I'd had the accident as a child, but had blotted out all memory of it, and certainly did not understand that the accident was responsible for the loss of certain faculties I had previously possessed. Nor did I realize that it accounted for an overall decline in cognitive skills. Described in the Prologue to *Deciphering the Golden Flower One Secret at a Time* – JJ Semple, Life Force Books, 2007.

17 Described on pg. 81 of *Deciphering the Golden Flower One Secret at a Time* – JJ Semple, Life Force Books, 2007.

18 *The Future of the Body* - Michael Murphy, Tarcher/Putnam, 1992, p. 37.

19 Ibid, p. 29.

20 *The Secret of the Golden Flower* – Routledge & Kegan Paul, Wilhelm Translation, p. 41.

21 Karl S. Kruszelnicki Pty Ltd 2003
These aren't a bunch of wild notions I just cooked up. There is a school of psychology that studies the effects of symmetry in everyday life. It's called Evolutionary Psychology and it researches the effect of individual symmetry on success, on talent, on beauty, on mutual attraction, on health. *See* http://findarticles.com/p/articles/mi_qn4159/is_20051002/ai_n15644767 and http://www.jyi.org/volumes/volume6/issue6/features/feng.html

22 Adrian Bruce–www.adrianbruce.com

23 *The Awakening of Kundalini* – Gopi Krishna, D. B. Taraporevala Sons & Company Private Ltd., Bombay, India, 1976, p. 103.

24 *The Secret of the Golden Flower* – Routledge & Kegan Paul, Wilhelm Translation, p. 35.

25 The "10,000 things" is the Taoist expression for interfering thoughts. Its many names include the Taoist expression: the 10,000 things as well as others, like the inner dialogue, monkey chatter—all the crazy, runaway mental activity that stifles our daily lives and interferes with meditation. Blocking the 10,000 things boils down to finding a means of calming mental activity during meditation.

26 Dr. Herbert Benson – The originator of the Relaxation Response.

27 *Deciphering the Golden Flower One Secret at a Time* – JJ Semple, Life Force Books, 2007.

28 "With regard to my question about reversing the breath: I must say that I appreciate your elaboration of the various dependencies here. Most importantly, though, your statement 'Once one does detect *the property* of movement or direction, it is possible to simply command [*emphasis mine*] the breath to reverse directions' is the clearest I've seen you put this. I did not realize it was simply a matter of *directed intention* rather than an actual 'doing.' Yes, I believe I now fully understand what you mean, even though I do not yet have my own experience with this method. Your elaboration here is so thorough that I feel like I know what I'd be looking for now, as well as what to do once I feel it. This makes me more comfortable about beginning the meditation practice."
    – Personal correspondence with Christine DeLuca.

29 *Deciphering the Golden Flower One Secret at a Time* – JJ Semple, Life Force Books, 2007.

30 Personal correspondence with Susan Grace.

31 Ibid

32 *Deciphering the Golden Flower One Secret at a Time* – JJ Semple, Life Force Books, 2007, p. 77.

33 The Brofman Foundation for the Advancement of Healing - http://www.healer.ch/browchakra.html

34 *Deciphering the Golden Flower One Secret at a Time* – JJ Semple, Life Force Books, 2007, p. 75.

35 Ibid, pg. 79.

36 "An ancient primer for practical godhead" – http://www.nine3.com/Magic.html

37 "An ancient primer for practical godhead" – http://www.nine3.com/Magic.html
    Once again, my contention about the danger of visualizing, "thinking," or forcing energy is upheld. Taoist methods rely a lot on practice—not

practicing in any old way, but following a progression of steps, relying on the body to respond in the correct manner, which when done while concentrating on the sensations, increases awareness. One becomes more adept at observation.

38 *The Fourth Way* – P. D. Ouspensky, Knopf, 1957.

39 *Deciphering the Golden Flower One Secret at a Time* – JJ Semple, Life Force Books, 2007, pp. 77-78.

40 http://www.npr.org/templates/story/story.php?storyId=18212250&ft= 1&f=3.

41 *The Secret of the Golden Flower* – Routledge & Kegan Paul, Wilhelm Translation, p. 42.

42 Ibid, p. 29.

43 *Reincarnation: The Missing Link in Christianity* – Elizabeth Clare Prophet, Summit University Press, 1997, p. 106.

44 *The Secret of the Golden Flower* – Routledge & Kegan Paul, Wilhelm Translation, p. 28.

45 *The Tibetan Book of the Dead* – WY Evans-Wentz, Oxford University Press, pp. 188 & 191.

46 Ibid, p. 192.

47 Ibid, p. 192.

48 Ibid, p. 192.

49 Based on "The Hymn of the Pearl." Layton, *The Gnostic Scriptures*, pp. 371-75.

50 *The Secret of the Golden Flower* – Routledge & Kegan Paul, Wilhelm Translation, p. 63.

51 *Evolution and Ethics* - T.H. Huxley, (London, 1894) pp. 61-62, 95 as quoted in *The Tibetan Book of the Dead* – Oxford University Press, WY Evans-Wentz, p. 61. "The late William James, the well-known American psychologist, independently arrived at substantially the same conclusion as Huxley; for, after explaining his 'own inability to accept either popular Christianity or scholastic theism,' he says, 'I am ignorant of Buddhism and speak under correction, and merely in order the better to describe my general point of view; but, as I apprehend the Buddhist doctrine of Karma, I agree in principle with that.' – (*The Variety of Religious Experience*, pp. 521-522.)

52 *The Universe in a Single Atom* - The Dalai Lama, Morgan Road Books, 2005.

53 *The Tibetan Book of the Dead* – WY Evans-Wentz, Oxford University Press, p. lxxvi.

54 *The Tibetan Book of the Dead* – WY Evans-Wentz, Oxford University Press, p. lxxxi. "The Science of Death" - Foreword by Sir John Woodroffe.

55 "The Pleasure Seekers" - Helen Phillips - http://www.thirdage.com/news/articles/ALT02/04/02/03/ALT02040203-02.html "Dopamine is closely associated with reward-seeking behaviors, such as approach, consumption, and addiction. Recent researchers suggest that the firing of dopaminergic neurons is a motivational substance as a consequence of reward-anticipation. This hypothesis is based on the evidence that when a reward is greater than expected, the firing of certain dopaminergic neurons increases, which consequently increases desire or motivation towards the reward." http://en.wikipedia.org/wiki/Dopamine

56 "The Unkindest Cut: The Science and Ethics of Castration" - Atul Gawande, *Slate Magazine*, Sunday, July 13, 1997.

57 "The Pleasure Seekers" - Helen Phillips - http://www.thirdage.com/news/articles/ALT02/04/02/03/ALT02040203-02.html

57 "A Cambodian Girl's Tragedy: Being Young and Pretty" – Nicholas Kristof, *The New York Times*, December 12, 2006.

58 "Murphy's 'Impossible Dream' of a Great Evolutionary Leap" – John Temple, Ascent, the Newsletter, 1992.

59 "Henry Miller Meets Gopi Krishna" – Amazon Review of *Deciphering the Golden Flower One Secret at a Time* - Dennis Littrell, Amazon Top 50 Reviewer, May 5, 2008.

60 Ibid.

61 "Qigong Meditation can produce astounding results" YouTube submission by "DeepKnowledge" July 30, 2007. http://www.youtube.com/watch?v=iM_E6sRQQAg

62 *Deciphering the Golden Flower One Secret at a Time* – JJ Semple, Life Force Books, 2007, p. 157.

63 Personal correspondence with Dennis Littrell, May 9, 2008.

64 "Information is Not Transformation" – Larry Dossey, *The Science of Sciences*, Chinmaya Publications, 2006.

65 "Science and Vedanta" – Swami Mukhyananda, *The Science of Sciences*, Chinmaya Publications, 2006.

66 *Kundalini: The Evolutionary Energy in Man* – Gopi Krishna, Shambala, 1971, p. 244.

67 *Deciphering the Golden Flower One Secret at a Time* – JJ Semple, Life Force Books, 2007, p. 146.

68 Personal correspondence with Dennis Littrell, May 9, 2008.

69 *The Awakening of Kundalini* – Gopi Krishna, D. B. Taraporevala Sons & Company, 1975, p. 105.

70 *Kundalini: The Evolutionary Energy in Man* – Gopi Krishna, Shambala, 1971, p. 102.

71 *The Awakening of Kundalini* – Gopi Krishna, D. B. Taraporevala Sons & Company, 1975, p. 103.

72 *The Biological Basis of Religion and Genius* – Gopi Krishna, Harper & Row, 1971, p. 92.

GLOSSARY

Backward-Flowing Method
The backward-flowing method is the Secret of Life. It awakens the Kundalini mechanism permanently and safely. Kundalini, in turn, activates the Life Force which then triggers a host of extraordinary metanormal effects, results, and responses in the human being.

Capitalization
You may have noticed that I capitalize terms like Kundalini, Life Force, Primal Spirit, Secret of Life. I do so out of respect for Nature and the natural elegance of its metaphysical phenomena.

Conscious Spirit
The Conscious Spirit is the perceiving mind. It is activated at birth, and then develops as the five senses explore the material world. It is schooled and conditioned in accordance to the cultural bias of its surroundings.

Dopamine
According to Wikipedia: "Dopamine is closely associated with reward-seeking behaviors, such as approach, consumption, and addiction. Recent researches suggest that the firing of dopaminergic neurons is a motivational substance as a consequence of reward-anticipation. This hypothesis is based on the evidence that when a reward is greater than expected, the firing of certain dopaminergic neurons increases, which consequently increases desire or motivation towards the reward."

Empirical science
In today's world we place so much value on classroom learning. In material science that is one thing, because students are trained to conduct and observe experiments. At least they are close to the reality they are trying to describe, even though they may not experience it. In other fields, classroom learning means research, i.e., second-hand learning. Little value is placed on observation and experience, what I call empirical science, which entails using your own body/being to add validity to a given hypothesis.

Extraordinary metanormal faculties
Includes faculties like out of body flying, clairvoyance, spontaneous language acquisition, prescience, and supernormal intelligence.

Golden Flower Meditation (GFM)
The method covered in this book. It is comprised of three steps: diaphragmatic deep breathing, control of heart rate, and backward-flowing method. Correctly applied, it will activate Kundalini.

Head & Body relationship
The shape of the head controls the shape of the body. I'm not sure if there has been any scientific research into this subject, but I have witnessed my body's size and shape change as the Life Force modified the shape of my head. The Life Force wants the body to be symmetrical so it will reshape the head to effect this. As a result, the body will change to reflect the shape of the head. In other words, the body cannot be symmetrical unless the head is.

Kundalini
There are already too many Kundalini definitions out there. I don't want to add to them. Rather let me quote Bruce Lee: "Knowing is not enough; we must apply. Willing is not enough; we must do." If you are interested in knowing about Kundalini read my books and the books of Gopi Krishna. You will probably learn something. The only real way to *know* Kundalini is by doing. Practice GFM.

Kundalini & gender
We speak of seminal fluid in the case of a man and cervical fluid in the case of a woman. When someone asks me if a woman can awaken Kundalini, I reply that I know of no anatomical reason precluding it. Nevertheless, I feel obligated to add that I don't know for sure because I am not a woman. Hope you don't feel this as a cop out. I would love to hear from women about this.

Kundalini-Life Force connection
Kundalini triggers the Life Force (the Primal Spirit). There is a cause and effect relationship between them.

Life Force Science
The science that investigates the effect of the Life Force on the individual being and on his or her life.

Material science
The investigation of the physical, material world.

Metanormal
Beyond the usual psychological, somatic, mental, and physical states. According to Michael Murphy, "Human functioning that in some respect radically surpasses the functioning of most people living today."

Metaphysical

Beyond the physical.

Morality and Kundalini

Becoming a better person begins with the purification of the body, the first priority of the Kundalini-Life Force process. Before activating Kundalini, you might not have paid much attention to the rational or moral aspects of your decisions. Kundalini induces you to consider the moral consequences of each decision and helps you realize that the Golden Rule applies in most cases.

Prana

There are many definitions of Prana that are better than mine. I've never isolated it in a laboratory; I've only felt its effect on my being. So working backwards, I'm inclined to say it's real.

Primal Spirit

Term for the Life Force in *The Secret of the Golden Flower*. They are interchangeable. There are many other terms for the Life Force that I don't care to include here because they will only confuse the issue. Again, if you haven't activated Kundalini, the definition of Primal Spirit or Life Force is of little consequence.

Secret of Life

See, *backward-flowing method.*

Secret Teachings

Those teachings that shed light on the true secrets of life, (e.g., the backward-flowing method).

Spiritual

I still don't have a definition. Send me yours.

Sublimation

The process of causing the seminal or cervical fluid to ascend the spinal column to the brain. Again, by *drawing* the fluid up the correct channel along the spine, the backward-flowing method assures this operation will be managed correctly.

Terminology

Terminology is the bane of so-called "spiritual" work. Writers are always trying to convert or transpose notions and phenomenon of the metaphysical plane into the terminology of the physical plane. There is no strict one-to-one equivalency. Terms are sometimes only describable by metaphor or example. Still, I believe that over time the metaphysical will become as palpable as the physical. A new vocabulary will arise as people begin to share the same metaphysical experiences, so they can be correlated.

INDEX